CITIZENSHIP EDUCATION FOR TERTIARY INSTITUTIONS

Kayode Asoga-Allen

REVISED EDITION

First published 2001

ISBN-13: 978-1534807396

www.kayodeasogaallen.com

FOREWORD

I feel honoured to write the foreword to Mr. Kayode Asoga Allen's book titled "Citizenship Education for Tertiary Institutions". The writing of the ten-chapter book is timely for two reasons: (i) The scarcity of good texts in the area.

(ii) The galvanizing effects of the book on effective teaching of General Studies in tertiary institution.

It is noteworthy that Mr. Asoga-Allen's wealth of experience in the teaching of Citizenship Education has influenced his mastery of the subject matter.

The book which begins with the concept of Citizen and Citizenship covers areas such as Constitution, Federation, Constituted Authority, Government, Arms of Government, Rights and Obligations, National Ethics and Discipline in National Life, National Identity, Nigerian Environment and some other useful readings.

The ability of the author to effectively intellectualize on all the key concepts and bring out cleanly facts that are valid for effective teaching and learning make the book a very worthy companion for all students and the reaching public. I therefore warmly recommend this text.

Professor 'Tunde Samuel
Former Provost, LACOPED,
Now MOCPED, Epe

PREFACE

The author has been encouraged to write this book by his several years of experience as lecturer of Citizenship Education in tertiary institution, and also by his practical experience as somebody who previously worked as an Education Officer with a Law Enforcement Agency in Nigeria. This book discusses in detail each of the topic in the course outline of Citizenship Education in tertiary institutions. It goes beyond mere discussion of facts relating to Citizenship Education, it highlights the limitations to certain issues e.g. fundamental human rights. This is necessary because there is a lot of erroneous ideas being held by most Africans concerning state governance, leadership, followership vis-à-vis rights and obligations of citizens. These erroneous ideas are brain children of ignorance. It has been discovered by the author that some people are in prison for an offence they did not commit deliberately but due to ignorance of the laws. As we all agree, ignorance is not an excuse in the Law court and an accused is presumed innocent until his case has been proved beyond all reasonable doubt.

It is important to stress that as a citizen of a nation; one must not only think about his rights, but also his obligations to the state. In Africa, everybody talks of rights, claims rights, and nobody ever remembered to talk of obligations. For a balanced society, rights and obligations must go pari-passu. It is true that one of the responsibilities of the government is to protect lives and properties, but It Is equally important to note that every man is the major protector of his rights. If you do not want your rights to be abused, you will respect the rights of others, because the moment you abuse the right of another person, you have committed an offence against the state, and in so doing, your rights or some of your rights may be tampered with. Thus, a citizen is only entitled to all his rights as stated in the Constitution of any nation only if he is law- abiding and abstains from anything that can implicate him.

This book is undoubtedly an asset to students of Colleges of Education, Polytechnics, Universities and the reading public in Nigeria. The importance of the book goes beyond making the prospective students pass their examinations creditably, it would also make them an enlightened and educated graduates who can differentiate their right hands from their left ones, and who are capable of facing the challenges of the society with all the seriousness it deserves, and completely be free from the bondage of dogmatism and ignorance.

I am highly grateful and doubly appreciative of the worthy contributions of those who have directly or indirectly contributed immensely to the successful completion of this book-particularly the various authors, writers, pamphleteers, commentators to mention a few, for the Indispensable pieces of information collected from their books, magazines, pamphlets, journals, periodicals, newspapers, etc as indicated in the reference section of this book.

Finally, I want to thank Mr. Viatonu Olumuyiwa (former Director, School of Part-Time Studies), Michael Otedola College of Primary Education and Dr. Olu Adesola Famade (former H.O.D. Educational Foundations and Management) now, a lecturer in the Faculty of Education, Adekunle Ajasin University, Akungba-Akoko, for the enlightenment and encouragement given to me when I came into academics newly. In fact, they have indeed, inspired me through their constant information and academic achievements.

Kayode Asoga-Allen

DEDICATION

This book is dedicated to the former Provost and Chief Executive of Lagos State College of Primary Education (LACOPED), now Michael Otedola College of Primary Education (MOCPED), Professor Tunde Samuel, for the opportunity and encouragement accorded me to function as academia, without his liberality and magnanimity, the dream would have died a natural death.

Table of Contents

14

15

CHAPTER ONE: The Concept of Citizen and Citizenship

Longman Dictionary of Contemporary English (1995) defines citizen as someone who lives in particular town, country or state who has rights and responsibilities there, or someone who belongs to a particular country whether he is living there or not. Citizenship therefore, refers to the legal right of belonging to a particular country. It is the status conferred on the individual who has full membership rights in the community (e.g. full economic, political, civil, social rights).

1.1   Types of Citizenship

Basically, citizenship can be classified into four main types, they include:

1. **Citizenship by Birth:** This is the type acquired through one's parents. In this regard if one's parents are from a country, the person automatically becomes a citizen of that country. For example, a child born to Nigerian parents automatically becomes a Nigerian citizen. Any child whose two parents belong to a country becomes a citizen of that country. This type of citizenship is referred to as blood citizenship and it is

the most recognized and probably the commonest type of citizenship.

2. **Citizenship by Naturalization:** This is the type of citizenship in which a person who has stayed in a country for years with good record and who has contributed something significant to the community which he lives, now put up an application for naturalization and if his application is granted, becomes a citizen by naturalization. Before a person could be naturalized:

(i)   He must have resided in the country for some years;

(ii)   He must be seen as an asset to the country rather than a liability;

(iii)   He must be acceptable to the local community that he/she has fully been assimilated into the way of life of the people;

(iv)   He must have contributed and be capable of contributing to the progress and development of the country;

(v)   He must apply through appropriate Ministry or Government Agency through the Governor or the State in which he/she lives.

3. **Citizenship by Registration:** This type of

citizenship is applicable to both men and women. A foreign woman who is married to a Nigerian husband can become a citizen of Nigeria through registration. Likewise, a foreign man that is married to a Nigeria wife becomes a citizen of Nigeria through registration. This is not peculiar to Nigeria alone, even countries like USA, UK, to mention a few, adopts citizenship by registration. The applicant must channel his/her application through the appropriate Ministry or Government Agency. Before such application is granted, the applicant must satisfy the Head of State that he/she is highly interested in Living in the country. Also, such an applicant must be ready to take an oath of allegiance to the country.

4. **Honorary Citizenship**: The government of a country may honour an eminent international political figure who has contributed significantly to the betterment of his people vis a vis international community with a honorary citizenship of that country. Examples of people who were honoured with honorary citizenship status of other countries include: Late Dr. Nelson Mandela who was an honorary citizen of Nigeria, Late Miriam Makeba, a South African, who had honorary membership of some African countries,

Late Chief M. K. O. Abiola who was a honorary citizen of United States of America.

1.2 Nigerian Citizenship

The constitutions of the Federal Republic of Nigeria (1960, 1963, 1979, 1992 and 1999) recognize three kinds of citizenship:

a)   Every person born in Nigeria before the date of independence either of whose parents or any of whose grandparents belong or belonged to community indigenous to Nigeria;

(b)   Every person born in Nigeria after the date independence either of whose parents or grandparents is a citizen of Nigeria; and

(c)   Every person born outside Nigeria either of whose parents is a citizen of Nigeria.

The 1979 and 1992 Constitutions also added the following conditions for Nigerian citizenship by naturalization and registration.

No person shall be qualified to apply for the grant of a certificate of naturalization, unless he satisfies the president that:

(a)   He is a person of full age and capacity;

(b)   He is a person of good character;

(c)   He has shown a clear intension of his desire to be domicile in Nigeria;

(d)   He is, in the opinion of the Governor of the State where he/she is or proposes to be resident, acceptable to the local community in which he is to live permanently, and has been assimilated into the way of life of Nigerians in that part of the federation;

(e)   He is a person who has made or is capable of making useful contribution to the advancement, progress and well-being of Nigeria;

(f)   He has taken the oath of allegiance prescribed in the seventh schedule of these constitutions;

(g)   He has, immediately preceding the date of his application, either:

       (i)   Resided in Nigeria for a continuous period of fifteen years or

       (ii)   Resident in Nigeria continuously for a period of twelve months, and during the period of twenty years immediately preceding that period of twelve months has resided in Nigeria for periods amounting in the aggregate to not less than fifteen years.

1.3   The Concept of Citizenship Education

Citizenship education has been defined by various scholars in various ways depending on the perspective of individual scholar defining it. Some of the definitions include Osakwe and Itedjere (1993) which defines citizenship education as the systematic process through which young people acquire or internalize the values, sentiments and norms of the society in which they live and actively get involved to ensure that the common good of the citizenship of the society is catered for; including resisting anti-social and unguided "youthful exuberance". He explained that citizenship education "involves critical thinking, political activism or inquiry plus the goals and values of a good citizen"

Ezegbe (1988) defines citizenship education as "that education through which pupils in the school system will be taught about their rights, privileges, duties and responsibilities as good citizens and through which they will be encouraged to seek such rights and privileges, perform their duties, and play a positive and active role in the society. Coleman (1965) in his effort to define citizenship education sees the subject as political socialization. According to him, it is a process by which individuals acquire attitude and feelings towards the political system and towards their roles in it. He outlines what the process involves as:

- Learning how the political system works;
- The growth of feelings (positive and negative) about the system; and
- Development or non-development of a sense of competence to participate actively in politics.

Citizenship education is an education given to the citizens of a nation to make them conscious of their rights, duties, responsibilities and obligations in the society as well as the expected roles of the government to the people. The governed needs be informed about the governmental activities, that is, the business of governance. And the governed owed it a duty to contribute or reciprocate the consultation by participating meaningfully and effectively in government by carrying out their obligations.

In any society, man constitutes the governmental structure, and elects those to represent them or their interests in government, especially in a democratic society. Every man has a role to play in the society both to ensure his continuity as well as to keep the governmental institutions functioning. Also, in every human society, there are rules and regulations. In Nigerian society, the constitution is the legal document on which governance is based. Citizenship education is more or less a political education or enlightenment of the citizens so as to make them good citizens who are free from the bondage of parochialism, ignorance and crudity. It is indubitable fact that no nation could attain greatness if the level of ignorance among its citizens assumes a major proportion. Citizenship education is not only an instrument for keeping the citizens informed about the governmental activities but also a means of liberating the citizens from the bondage of parochialism, self-centeredness, ethnicity, hooliganism, thuggery, favouritism, tribalism, bribery and corruption, putting one's interest above the national interest, injustice, cruelty, oppression and so on and so forth by equipping them with the pre-requisite knowledge that would enable them to play their role effectively and efficiently in their efforts to contribute their quotas to the national growth and upliftment. As Nierneyer (1957) rightly pointed out, citizenship education is to help children to be socially intelligent members of their community. Citizenship education finds its best application in the social context and involves acquisition of knowledge, attitudes and skills which will be utilized for the overall benefit of the society (Nwanyanwu, 1977).

It is expected that citizens who have passed through citizenship education should be able to:

i. Be conscious of their rights and the rights of others;

ii. Be able to function effectively and efficiently in any governmental institution;

iii. Possess and demonstrate political knowledge;

iv. Be loyal and patriotic;

v. Put national interest above the self-interest;

vi. Be highly disciplined;

vii. Interact freely with the various ethnic groups in the county;

viii. Respect the constitution of the Federal Republic of Nigeria;

ix. Be nationalistic in approach rather than tribalistic; and

x. Make accountability and probity their watchword in both private and public lives.

1.4 The National Objectives of Citizenship Education

The national objectives of citizenship education in Nigeria include:

a) To create awareness of the Nigerian constitution and the need for democracy in Nigeria;

b) To acquaint Nigerians with the functions and obligations of the government;

c) To create adequate functional political literacy among the people;

d) To make Nigerians fully conscious of their rights, duties and obligations and to respect the rights of others;

e) To assist in the production of responsible, well-informed and self-reliant Nigerian citizens.;

f) To inculcate the right values e.g. honesty, integrity, hard work, faithfulness, fairness and justice. To foster attitudes of togetherness, comradeship and cooperation among the various people of Nigeria;

g) To inculcate the concept of authority, leadership and followership into the citizens;

h) To produce citizens who are capable of participating meaningfully in discussions on the Nigerian system of government and electoral process, arms of government, code of conduct for public officers and the roles of mass media in national development;

i) To articulate our history, national symbols, people and cultures of Nigeria; and

j) To discuss the characteristics features of the Nigerian environment as well as the roles of national and international conservation agencies.

These national objectives were based on the fact that civics which was being taught in Nigerian schools before the advent of citizenship education tended to make Nigeria citizens more conscious of foreign affairs than their indigenous national affairs, and this was found to be inadequate for an independent country like Nigeria. The content of civics was merely the dos and don'ts of the society which aims were to produce good boys and girls. With the evolution of citizenship education, "civics" stopped to exist. The objectives of citizenship education are wide and the content cut across all segments of man to man relationship, man to government relationship, institution to institution relationship, in fact, that knowledge that man needs to function as an intelligent, effective and efficient member of his society. Unlike other subjects in the curriculum of our schools, knowledge of citizenship education is something that man needs throughout his life time if he wants to live a peaceful and crises free life.

Ignorance is not an excuse in the law court, man needs to be informed and be properly informed so as not to be in the dark. No amount is too much for a nation to educate its citizens. This is so because ignorance is more expensive than education. The laws are made not to trap man but to instil obedience. When laws are made and the citizens that the laws are made for are not informed about the existence of such laws until they become victims, the laws become unjustifiable in the court of natural justice. Laws are undoubtedly indispensable instruments for controlling human behaviour, to ensure that everybody works towards the attainment of societal goals and objectives, since any negative behaviour on the part of the citizens might be detrimental and harmful to the attainment of the societal goals, objectives and the needed peace and orderliness.

CHAPTER TWO: CONSTITUTION

In every human society, there is need for orderliness; also there are things which the society regards as good or bad. Every society encourages its people to do that which the society approves and discourages that which the society feels are bad and harmful to the peaceful existence of that society. It is important to note that what a society regards as good and acceptable behaviour may not be the same with all what another society regards as same. This is as a result of cultural differences of one society from another. That is to say that every society has its own peculiar way of life which is a product of evolution. This way of life of a people is referred to as culture.

The cultural ways of a society comprises of dos and don'ts. Just as the acceptable behaviours are rewarded in human society bad behaviours are punished or sanctioned. In order to make people conscious of what they should do and what they should not do, and the penalties for unruly behaviour there is always a constitution.

Constitution is therefore a set of rules and regulations governing the activities of the government and the governed. It consists of information about what should be done and how to do it as well as penalties for contravening any item of the constitutional provisions. A state or nation's constitution always addresses certain fundamental questions such as:

(a) Who is the executive, legislative and judiciary?

(b) How are they recruited and when do they leave office?

(c) What type of government do a state runs and what are the arms of government?

(d) Who is a citizen, a foreigner and what rights do they have?

(e) What power does each arm of government has? Is this power autonomous?

(f) What type of constitution is operated (written or unwritten) and how does the constitution gets changed? And so on and so forth.

2.1 Classification of Constitution

Constitution can be classified into basically four categories, namely, written constitution, unwritten constitution, unitary constitution and federal constitution:

1. **Written Constitution**

A written constitution is the one that is

contained in a particular document. This document has been compiled at a particular time and place containing all the fundamental laws of how the people of a given country are governed or principles on which the government operates, establishing all the institutions of government and the powers belonging to each. Examples of countries with written constitution include: Nigeria, Sierra Leone, USA, USSR, Ghana, Gambia and so on and so forth.

2. **Unwritten Constitution**

This simply means a constitution that is not documented or contained in a particular document. In this type of constitution, the laws according to how a state is governed are not put into black and white. An example of country with unwritten constitution is UK. British constitution is more or less a historic evolution, drawn from diverse sources. Though, some parts of the British constitution have been written down while other parts are left unwritten down up till date.

3. **Unitary Constitution**

This is a type of constitution in which the

central government is supreme over other levels of government. It is a major centre of power, that is, power comes from the centre only. Other levels of government derive their governmental powers from the central authority and such power could be taken from them should the central/national government decides to do so. In essence, the local or state government have not derived their governmental or administrative powers from the constitution. Rather, it has been given to them by the central government. Some of the countries operating unitary constitution include Ghana, United Kingdom and so on and so forth.

4. **Federal Constitution**

In this type of constitution the governmental power are shared between the various levels of government. That is, the power exercisable by each level of government is derived from the constitution. Both the federal, state and local governments are autonomous in discharging their constitutional functions. No level of government has the right to usurp the power of another level of government. One important thing with the federal constitution or federal system of government is that each component state, like its central government, has its own complete system of governmental institutions. For example just as there is executive, legislative and judiciary at the federal or central level, the same thing we have the executive, legislative and judiciary at the state and local levels.

2.2   Types of Constitution

Basically, there are two types of constitution namely, flexible and rigid constitutions:

(a)   **Flexible Constitutions:** These are the constitutions in which the fundamental laws can easily be changed or amended without necessarily passing through the normal law making processes e.g. unwritten British constitution. It is importance to stress that a constitution may be written and at the same time remain flexible e.g. the case of New Zealand, Italy and Ghana especially during the first republic constitutions.

(b)   **Rigid Constitution:** When a constitution is rigid, it simply means that the fundamental laws contained in the constitution cannot be changed easily. If at all, it would be changed, it has to be subjected to the normal law making process. The changing processes are usually stated in the constitution. Examples of countries whose constitutions are rigid include the following: Australia, Switzerland, Canada, USA, and Nigeria to mention a few. Rigid constitutions are usually written.

2.3 Advantages of Written Constitution

The following are the advantages of written constitution:

1. It is usually on a single document which indicates the duties of the government and the rights of the citizens.

2. It cans only be amended in a definite manner or procedure.

3. Relevant parts of the constitution can be quoted to support argument in the court of law.

4. It enhances the possibility of administration of justice and makes it possible for citizens to have a fair judgment in the law court.

5. Perversion of justice can easily be detected. This is because any judgment pronounced that is not in accordance with the written

constitution would easily be faulted and hence, appealed against

6. It enables both the government and the governed to know their rights and duties as laid down in the constitution; hence citizens can take the government up in the law court in case of violation, infringement/abuse of their rights.

2.4 Disadvantages of Written Constitution

Written constitution has the following disadvantages:

1. It gets obsolete quickly due to the fact that the society is not static but dynamic
2. The amendment may be cumbersome since it has to be subjected to the law making process
3. It may hamper quick decision of government
4. The youth may challenge its operation due to generation gap
5. It may develop into tradition with time.

2.5 Advantages of Unwritten Constitution

1. It promotes quick decision making
2. It is adaptable to situations
3. It does not become outdated

4. It is rarely liable to youth resistance
5. It springs out from actual experiences of the people
6. It is relevant to societal situation

2.6 Disadvantages of Unwritten Constitution

1. Reference cannot be made to it in the court of law
2. It is rarely relevant in a large nation made up of several ethnic groups with different cultures.
3. It can promote perversion of justice
4. It can produce criminally minded people
5. Citizens may be ignorant of their rights
6. It may be used by dictatorship to further his political ambition.
7. It could be used as an instrument of oppression

2.7 Advantages of Rigid Constitution

1. It could ensure policy stability
2. It may disallow dictatorship tendencies as haste alterations are not possible
3. Fundamental rights are guaranteed and protected

4.   It makes continuity possible

2.8   Disadvantages of Rigid Constitution

1.   It is not suitable for emergency situations
2.   Over-abrogation of too much power to the judiciary
3.   It could elicit revolution
4.   It is bureaucratically cumbersome

2.9   Advantages of Flexible Constitution

1.   It is suitable for emergency cases
2.   It allows for quick decision
3.   Outdated laws could be easily replaced
4.   It is less expensive to change

2.10 Disadvantages of Flexible Constitution

1.   It cannot meet the needs of societies with multi-ethnic groups and culture
2.   It could be used by leaders to perpetuate their dictatorship tendencies
3.   It could cause political instability

2.11 Historical Development of Constitution in Nigeria

In the year 1914, Lord Lugard amalgamated the Northern Nigeria, the Colony and the Protectorate of Southern Nigeria and Lugard emerged the Governor-General. Lagos Colony was put under the control of an administrator while Northern and the Southern Provinces were administered respectively by Lieutenant-Governors. The Nigerian Council made of the representatives from the North and four representatives from south was set up by Lord Lugard. This Council provided the avenue for discussing affairs of Nigeria as nation under a Governor Lord Lugard. Members of the Council acted at advisory level as they were elected.

For the purpose of clarity, the historical development of Nigerian constitution can be divided into the following stages:

1.   The pre-independence constitutional development era (1914-1959)
2.   The independence constitutional development era (1960)
3.   The post-independence constitutional development (1961-1999)

2.12 The Pre-independence Constitutional Development Era (1914-1959)

The constitutions developed at this period include

(a) The 1914 Lugard Constitution

(b) The 1922 Clifford Constitution

(c) The 1939 Bourdillon Constitution

(d) The 1946 Richard Constitution

(e) The 1951 Macpherson Constitution

(f) The 1954 Lyttleton Constitution

(g) The 1957/58 Constitutional Conference

2.13 Lugard Constitution (1914)

Only the Lugard Constitution of 1914 combined legislative and executive functions. All others separated them. Clifford Constitution of 1922 consisted of 46 members, 26 whites, 15 non-officials nominated by the Governor, 4 elected Africans and Governor Clifford as the President. The importance of Clifford Constitution was that it allowed for election of members and more Africans were represented in the Council.

The weakness of Clifford Constitution includes:

(a)   Non-inclusion of African in the executive

(b)   The North was neglected

(c)   Whites majority or dominance

2.14 Sir Bernard Bourdillon Constitution (1939)

Sir Bernard Bourdillon was Governor of Nigeria between 1939 and 1943. The Bourdillon Constitution proposed:

(a)   Increased number of Africans in superior posts in the civil service.

(b)   Increased responsibility of native administration and

(c)   Unofficial Africans in the central legislature. Bourdillon was yet to implement these ideas before he left office.

2.15 Richard Constitution

Sir Richard became Governor of Nigeria in 1946 at exactly the time the 1946 Constitution was being drafted, and therefore the Constitution was named after him.

The Objectives of this constitution include:

(a)   To increase participation of Nigerians in the affairs of Nigeria

(b)   To foster unity of Nigeria by a representative

system of government

(c)   Dividing Nigeria into North, South and east to be administered by Chief Commissioner respectively and

(d)   To promote political and constitutional links between native authorities and the legislative council.

The main features of the Richard's Constitution were: legislative council, regionalism and executive council. The legislative council comprised of non-officials as majority. Regionalism made it possible for the North, the West and the East to have their own legislative councils. The executive council as feature of the Richard's constitution made provision for the Secretary of state of the colonies to recommend the appointment of its members (the Chief Secretary, Regional Chief Commissioners, the Attorney-General, the Finance Secretary, the Director of Medical Services, the Director of Education) to be appointed by the Governor.

Richard's constitution made the following achievements:

(a)   It increased participation of Nigerians in the colonial administration.

(b)   It brought together the North and South under one legislative council

(c)   It established Regions and Regional Council

(d)   It established link between the native and legislative authorities

The defects of Richard's constitution include:

(i)   Regional assemblies could only discuss their own affairs but not Nigerian affairs

(ii)   The Governor or Chiefs nominated majority of the unofficial

(iii)   Franchise was limited to Lagos and Calabar

2.16 MacPherson Constitution (1951)

(a)   MacPherson Constitution could be said to be democratic in that it involved Nigerians at all levels (villages, districts provinces and regions) in the drafting of the constitution.

(b)   A House of Representatives was created. This was the Council of Ministry drawn from each of the 3 regions. The house was charged with the responsibility of making laws for the whole country.

(c)   Each regional council depended heavily on the central council.

(d)   The Western and Northern regions had House of Assembly and the House of Chiefs, while the East had only House of Assembly

(e)   The ministers both at the Central and Regional levels were purely Nigerians.

(f)   There was revenue allocated formula initiated between central and the regions.

2.17 Disadvantages of Macpherson Constitution

1.   It over-concentrated too much power in the hands of the Governor.

2.   There was no accepted nationwide party that could control majority at the central government

3.   Projects could not be financed at the regional level due to inability to raise revenue.

The struggle for self-determination started in 1956 and was championed by Chief Enahoro, Action Group member. The representatives of the North in the Assembly did not support the move toward self-determination or political independence. This led to their leaving Lagos for the North. This was followed with a threat by the North to secede. In 1953 Chief S.L. Akintola led a team of Action Group (AG) men to campaign in the North and this led to the kano riots of 1953. Many southerners lost their lives and properties in the North.

2.18 The Lyttleton Constitution (1954)

The Lyttleton Constitution of 1954 emerged out of the London and Lagos Conferences of 1953 and 1954. All the three regions were adequately represented at the conferences.

The major features of the Lyttleton constitution included:

1. Premiers were appointed instead of Prime Ministers for each Region.
2. There was creation of office of the speaker.
3. Electoral laws were made by each Region.
4. It retained the three Regions.
5. Powers were specified into exclusive, concurrent and residual lists. Exclusive list was exercised exclusively by the Federal Government; the concurrent list on the other hand, was exercised by both the Federal and Regional while Residual list was reserved for the Regional Government.
6. In 1954, the first general election was held.

2.19 The 1957/1958 Constitutional Conference

The 1957/58 Constitution Conference came up in London. The following vital decisions were taken at the conference:

1. House of Chiefs was to be granted to the East, the West and the North.
2. Bi-cameral legislature to be introduced at the centre.
3. Basic human rights to be spelt out.
4. Nigeria independent was proposed to 1st October, 1960.
5. Cameroun to be accorded Regional status.
6. The Police Force was to be put on the exclusive list.
7. The West and East should be independent 1957 while North should be independent in 1959.

Sir Abubakar Tafawa Balewa emerged as the Federal Minister as a result of the coalition government formed by the Northern People Congregation (NPC) and the National Council of Nigeria and the Cameroun (NCNC). The Action Group (AG) became the opposition party and late Chief Obafemi Awolowo became the opposition leader. Dr Nnamdi Azikwe emerged the first Governor -General in 1960.

2.20 The Independence Constitutional Development Era (1960)

Nigeria obtained political independent on the 1st of October, 1960 and the 1960 Independent Constitution came into operation from the date of independence.

The provisions of the constitution include:

a. A Governor General who was to represent Queen of England only.

b. A Prime Minister was to be the Head of Government

c. Regional Governors were to appoint their respective Premiers

d. Division of power to exclusive, concurrent and residual

e. There was to be bi-cameral legislature at both federal and regional levels.

f. Appeals could go from Regional judiciary to the Federal and finally to Privy Council in London

g. Fundamental human rights were enumerated

h. Provision was made for state of emergency

i. State creation was to be by majority approval

2.21 The Post-Independence Constitutional Development Era (1961-1999)

In 1963 Nigeria became a Republic and this was followed with a Republic Constitution. The constitution made the following provisions:

The position of Governor General was to be replaced with that of President who was to be constitution Head of State. He was appointed by the House of Representatives and the Senate. His tenure of office was put at 5 years.

The second republican constitution (1979)

A special committee known as Constitutional Drafting Committee (CDC) was set up in 1975 and was chaired by Chief Rotimi Williams. It was charged with the responsibility of drafting a new constitution for Nigeria's second republic.

The provisions of this constitution include:

a. The adoption of the executive presidential system that was Head of State and Commander in-Chief of the Armed Forces.

b. President must be appointed by 2/3 majority.

c. Election of State Governor or Gubernatorial candidate.

d.   Separation of Powers.

e.   President to be accountable to the people.

f.   Impeachment and lobbying are special instrument of governance and

g.   Provision for basic Human Rights

CHAPTER THREE: FEDERATION

Any country that practices federal constitution is a federation. And its government is usually referred to as a federal system of government.

Federalism is a system of government in which the governmental powers are shared between all the tiers of government. That is, between federal, state and local government. In this case, each of the tiers of government derives its governmental powers directly from the constitution and enjoys a high degree or magnitude of autonomy in exercising its legitimate powers. Unlike the situation with the unitary system of government where power is concentrated only at the centre, and other tiers of government derive their powers from the central government and the central government can seize the power given to the other tiers when it feels like doing so. With the federal system of government, no level of government has right to seize the power given to another tier of government or usurp her function.

Federalism could also be seen as a group of neighbouring separate states who hitherto enjoyed full autonomy, now decided to come together under one umbrella to form a larger country and set up a single central government to rule the new larger state. The states being conscious of their cultural differences and identities surrendered only part of their governmental powers to the central government and retain some parts.

Federalism is usually the case in societies or states where the people are not willing to surrender all their powers to a central authority. Federalism makes it possible for the United States to enjoy common security, currencies, trade, and communication and to pursue issues of common interest. An example of a country with federal system of government is Nigeria. The Federal Republic of Nigeria is made up of 36 states and Abuja the Federal Capital.

3.1   Reasons for the Adoption of Federal System of Government in Nigeria

Federalism was adopted in Nigeria for a number of reasons, these include:

(a)   **Economic reason**

It is true that Nigeria is blessed with abundant natural resources however, it is important to note that these natural resources are not equitably distributed throughout Nigeria. In essence, the regions that make up Nigeria are economically different from one another. The products of the southern part of Nigeria are different from that of the north; while eastern states are rich in crude oil, the northern states do not have crude oil but rich in agricultural resources. The level of development among the various regions is not the same. But for the purpose of equal development and advantages in unity, the people decided to adopt a federal system of government.

(b) **Cultural differences**

Nigeria is made up of various ethnic groups and culture, People are culturally different in terms of their language, belief, custom, dress and food. To take care of every culture and ethnic group interest, federal system of government was adopted. This is so because federalism allows for equal representation of every ethnic regions in government and allows every tribe to have a sense of belonging.

(c) **Administrative effectiveness and efficiency**

Nigeria is a large country covering a vast land. Nigeria has a territory covering about 925, 000 sq kms and according to census (1912) a population of about 168.8million. From North to South, it is approximately 1,300 kms and about 1,100 kms East to West. The country is so large that any centralization of power could not bring about an effective and efficient administration. That is, the needs of the people would rarely be adequately met with a single administrative unit for the whole country. Thus, there is need to decentralize power for the purpose of making government presence felt in all nooks and crannies of the country.

(d) **Fear of domination**

In Nigeria, there are major and minority ethnic groups. The fear of the minority ethnic groups was that if power is concentrated in the centre, there is the possibility of someone from the majority ethnic group emerging as the nation's ruler and monopolise power at the detriment of the minority group. In essence, that people from the minority group may not have the fair share of the national cake. Thus, the minority ethnic groups demanded for autonomous government that could only be guaranteed by the federal form of government.

(e) **Historical reason**

It is factual that there had been some sort of conflict between one ethnic group or the other before the advent of the British colonialists. These conflicts that arose from issues ranging from political, economic, religious and social, did a lot of harm to the unity of the people until after the British colonialists came. When the British came they united the people most especially through the amalgamation of the Northern and Southern Protectorates in 1914 by Lord Lugard, to form a country under a single central government. The taste of unity which the people had during the colonial days made the federal system of government the best alternative to them. As the people were unwilling to separate from one another or to be united under one single government.

(f) **Geographical closeness**

The geographical terrain of Nigeria made it possible for the ethnic groups or states to have unit of diverse society. The geographical terrain made a common territory possible between one ethnic group and another. And this makes easy flow of communication between one ethnic region and another. It would have been difficult if not impossible, if there is communication barrier between one ethnic group and another or if people would have to travel some kilometers before getting to one another.

3.2   Characteristics of Federation

Certain features are common to all countries or states adopting a federal system of government. These features include:

a.   Supremacy of the constitution. The constitution is supreme to all the tiers of government. None of the governments be it federal, state or region has the right to amend or ignore the constitution for any personal reason or selfish interest.

b.   The central government (federal) is supreme to all other levels of government is case of conflicts. Though they both derived their powers from the constitution but where there is a conflict between the state and central government, certain powers are conferred on the central government (exclusive power) while others are left with residual powers.

c.   Bi-cameral legislature: There is usually two

houses in the legislature, these are House of Representatives and house of senates.

d. Right to break away by states or regions are disallowed except in former USSR.

e. The judiciary is independent and is charged with the duties of interpreting the constitution and settles disputes

3.3 Introduction of the Nigerian Federal System

The genesis of federation in Nigeria could be traced to the Richard's Constitution of 1946. Federalism was actualized in Nigeria In 1954, but the idea for its introduction was born by the Richard's Constitution. Initially, the Nigerian federalism was based on three regional structures, namely, the North, West and East. The fourth region which is the Mid-Western region was added in 1963. General Gowon Who was a military head of state in Nigeria created twelve (12) states out of the four (4) regions. Other rulers of the country that created more states include General Murtala Muhammed in 1975, who Increased the 12 states to 19 states and General Ibrahim Gbadamosi Babangida who created nine (9) states in 1991. However, as at today, the Federal Republic of Nigeria is made up of thirty-six (36) states structures with Abuja as the Federal Capital.

3.4 Structure of the Nigeria Federal System

Nigerian federal system is made up of the following structures:

(a) **The Supreme Court**

This is responsible for giving final interpretation of the constitution. It is the nation's highest court. Whatever interpretation given by the supreme court must be acceptable to the federal, state or local government in case of any dispute. It is headed by the Chief Justice of the Federation and Justices of the Supreme Court. The appointment of these judges is made by the President and approved by the legislatures.

(b) **The Senate**

This is made up of two house chambers, the lower house and the upper house. The senate is expected to be made up of politicians who have subjected their personal interest to the national interest. Politicians who see their appointments as an opportunity to contribute their quotas to the upliftment of their fatherland as against tribalistic, selfish and unscrupulous politicians. The senate (upper chamber) helps in reducing the burden of work at the lower chamber (House of Representatives). They acts as a check on the activities of the House of Representatives as regards passing of bills. They ensure that no bill is passed hastily by the House of Representatives.

(c) **The Federal Civil Service**

The federal civil service is made up of various ministries each headed by a Minister. The post of Minister is a political one. Next to the minister is the Permanent Secretary, who is expected to be a career civil servant. At a time in Nigeria, the permanent secretaries were the administrative and accounting heads of the ministries. However, as from 1990, the ministers became both the political and accounting officers and the position of Director General was introduced to replace that of the Permanent Secretary. And the appointment of Director- General was made political like that of the Minister, however with the evolution of the third republic, the position of Director-

General has been replaced with that of Permanent Secretary.

3.5 Relationship between the Various Units of the Federal System in Nigeria

At the initial stage, the federation of Nigeria was made up of two levels of government (federal and regions and later states). The relationship between the two at the beginning was not cordial as the relationship looked like that of superior/subordinates. Both seemed to see each other as rivals rather than partners in progress. However, with the 1976 local government reforms, the relationship between federal, states and local governments could be said to have improved significantly. Rather than the previous one in which they both see each Other as rivals, they now see each other as partners in progress. Though, that is not to say that the relationship has been smooth at all times, there are instances when misunderstanding erupted between them and they dragged each other to court.

The federal government is seen as superior in status, followed by the states and then the local government. The federal government allocates funds to the local governments and the states. 20% of the federally generated revenue are allocated to local governments while states allocates 5% of its generated revenue to all the local Governments within its territory.

3.6 A Comparative Study of Other Federations — USA and USSR

Other countries of the world practicing a federal system of government include: USA, USSR, Federal German Republic, Austria and Switzerland. When it comes to sharing of powers and functions; the following are noticeable in USA and USSR's federations:

S/N	USA Federation	USSR
1	It is less centralized with considerable legislative and executive powers.	It is more centralized with most of the governmental powers resting with the Federal Government.
2	It favour multi or bi-party system.	It adopts one party system.
3	The right to break away is not allowed	The right to break away is allowed and this accounted for the breaking of the former

		USSR into many countries in 1995.
4	It has Federal constitution which is documented and stipulates the functions of each level of Government	It has Federal constitution which is documented and stipulates the function of each level of Government.
5	It operates a bi-cameral legislature and a supreme court.	It operates a bi-cameral legislature and a supreme court.
6	More Federal than USSR	Less Federal than USA

It is important to note that the differences in both federations are due to differences in political ideologies.

CHAPTER FOUR: CONSTITUTED AUTHORITY

A constituted authority can be defined as an authority that has the legal backing of the constitution. It is an authority constituted in line with the existing rules and regulations guiding the constitution of such authority in the society.

It is an authority in which both the leaders and followers are not left in doubt as to what is expected of them at a given point in time as a result of the legality of the authority. In a constituted authority, the source of authority is well known to the followers and they obey the authority willingly, there is no need for enforcing obedience. Constituted authority is necessary in every human society for Orderliness, progress and peaceful co-existence of the people. It is also necessary in a large society where there are specialized Institutions to carry out the activities for its survival.

4.1   Types of Constituted Authority

The following are examples of constituted authority:

1.   Constituted authority in educational institutions.

2. Constituted authority in ministries and parastatals
3. Constituted authority in houses of worship.
4. Constituted authority in the Army/Navy/Police
5. The President of a country and his Cabinet
6. The Governor of a state and his Cabinet
7. The Local Government Chairman and his Cabinet etc.

It is pertinent to note that, within a constituted authority there are likely to be sub-constituted authorities, for example, in the University System or College of Education, the major constituted authorities are the Vice-Chancellor or Provost as the academic head and the Registrar as the administrative head. Other important positions that could be said to be major include that of the Librarian and the Bursar. Under each of these constituted authorities, there are others that could be regarded as sub-constituted authorities for example, take the Vice-Chancellor or the Provost as an academic head of the institution, next to him are the Deans of Faculties/Schools, next to the Deans of Schools, are the Heads of Departments, before coming to the Lecturers.

To the students, even the lecturers are constituted

authorities because they are legally employed and given functions to perform. This is so because, when a lecturer gives instruction concerning the legitimate teaching and learning of his course, the instruction has to be obeyed by the students without hesitation, because he is an authority constituted for that purpose.

At this juncture, one may rightly say that anyone who is legally charged with the responsibility of carrying out a specified function to the public by a constituted authority is also a constituted authority.

4.2   Power and Authority

Power may be defined as the ability or capability to dominate others by making them do one's will. It is the ability to achieve ones interest on other people. Every human being has self-interest in most cases; one would want his interest to prevail under certain conditions. For example, the interest of an armed robber who enters into another man's house to attack him is to disown him of his money and valuables. He would want to achieve this on whoever he attacks by the use of force or coercion. The self-interest of a child among his peer group is to dominate them and give instruction to others and make them obey. He achieves this by threatening to beat up whoever disobeys his instruction. As he fought one or two of them before and defeated them, this defeat would automatically make other to fear him and would go a long way in making them obey him.

In a power situation, there are usually two categories of people, the person exercising the power and the person(s) whom the power is being exercised upon. The person whom the power is being exercised upon may have to obey for the fear of punishment. For example, a boy who enticed a girl to his house and after getting there armed himself with a knife and demanded sex from the girl; he asked the girl to cooperate or be killed. Under normal circumstances, the girl would not have accepted such demand but for the fear of punishment, the lady had to comply. The lady complied unwillingly therefore; she was forced against her will. In this type of situation, what the boy used against the girl is power.

Another example is a boy who asked his friend to give him his biro or be beaten mercilessly. If his friend obeyed that instruction and gave him the biro perhaps, the boy is stronger than him, what the boy used over his friend is power. When you make people do what is not their will because of the threat of being punished in case they do otherwise, you are using power.

Power can be classified into two namely, legitimate and illegitimate power. A legitimate power is the type exercised by a person who is authorized to do so. For example, the power exercised by a democratically elected president, Governor, Chairman etc is a legitimate power because he has the authority to do so. The authority in this sense is the mandate given to him by the masses who voted him to power.

An illegitimate power is the type being exercised by somebody without the authority of the people. It is the type of power that is not backed up or lack the support of the constitution. In the real sense, illegitimate power is unconstitutional and it usually emanates from the selfish interest of the person using it. An example of illegitimate power is the type exercised by military head of states or military in governance. This so because the traditional or primary duties of the military as contained in the constitution of the Federal Republic of Nigeria or any nation does not include to rule or govern.

Authority deals with the probability that a given set of instructions or orders would be obeyed or carried out by a targeted audience because they are convinced that they should obey. The conviction in this sense is the fact that people are conscious of the source of the authority. It can also be seen as the mandate given by the masses to a democratically elected person or a person appointed according to the constitution. The conviction to obey the authority is also due to the fact that people participated in ordaining that authority. Thus, in an authority situation, people do not bother themselves with the rightness or wrongness of the order or instruction because they know the source. That is to say that people comply willingly in an authority situation. The use of threat, coercion or force that use to accompany illegitimate power situation are completely absent in authority situation. Whoever disobeys the authority would be condemned by the society that is, the existing laws guiding against such behaviour not necessarily the person that dish out the order as it is the case with power situation.

It is possible for power situation to become an authority one especially when the person exercising the power now decides to do what the people want. An example was Colonel Mohammed Buba Marwa, who was a Military Administrator of Lagos State, because of his excellent performance in the state; the people of the state love his administration and even wanted him to continue to rule them. In that situation, his power has been legitimized. That is, his power had become authority.

Authority in its own case would ever remain an authority. However, it is important to say that authority is power-oriented or laden. That is, when you have authority, it automatically gives you power to act at the level of the authority.

A person elected as Governor has the power to carry out all the functions attached to the position of the Governor likewise, a person elected as President, or Local Government Chairman. Also, when you are appointed or employed to act at any capacity, that appointment goes with authority and power to discharge your functions. In all, there can be power without authority but there is no authority without power.

4.3   Elements of Power

Basically, these are those things that constitute power or that could be regarded as ingredients of power — for an individual or nation.

(a)   **Population / Followership**

A person who has 50 persons as members of his family is expected to be stronger than another person whose members are ten. Also, a country that has a population of 40 million people is expected to be stronger than a country with 20 million people, more so when the bulk of the population falls between 18-45 years.

(b)   **Geographical location**

The geographical location of a country or state constitutes an important element of its power. A country that is easy to penetrate would be prone to attack than a country that has a difficult terrain e.g. forest, Iceland, mountains etc.

(c)   **Technology**

Technology aids industrialization. It includes discovery, manufacturing and maintenance of weapons. An industrialized country that is capable of manufacturing weapons would be stronger than a country that buys weapons. Those countries regarded as the super power in the world today e.g. USA, USSR, Britain, France, etc owe much to their technological advancement.

(d)   **Economic resources**

This also determines the source and an extent of power. A very rich country would be stronger than a poor country. America is able to control the world today due to abundant resources at her disposal from which she gives aids to other countries. Without money nothing can be done, whoever is rich whether country or individual would be stronger than a poor country or individual.

(e)   **Military and intelligence agencies**

A country where military is professionalized, and people study warfarism in military institutions would be stronger than a nation where people are just recruited into the army and trained for six months and that is all. Also, when a country developed her intelligence agencies with tentacles in many parts of the world such a country cannot be compared with those with poorly developed or no institutionalised intelligence agencies. An example of countries with highly developed intelligence agencies and institutions are USA, Britain and so on and so forth.

(f)   **Diplomacy and leadership**

Every nation of the world engages in diplomacy. In that, they have their embassies in many countries of the world. The essence of this is to market their countries potentials in those countries and to engage those countries in political, economic and social manoeuvring when need be. Those countries that are good at diplomacy are stronger than those with poor diplomacy. Also, the ability of any person or country to take leadership position among other nations or committees of nations will to some extent depend on the quality of her diplomacy and leadership

4.4   Leadership and Followership

In every human society, there must be leadership and followership. This is a necessity for the purpose of cooperation, orderliness and smooth existence and co-existence of the people with one another and with the society at large. Not all can become leader; some must be leading while others must be following in the society. Leadership may simply be defined as the ability to lead while followership simply means giving support to somebody that leads or following a leader. For one to become a leader, he must possess certain leadership qualities. These qualities include being firm, being highly principled, being tolerant, being patriotic, being sympathetic, being honest, being intelligent, possession of verbal skills, being of high Integrity and dignity, being adaptable and being caring.

A leader must not be self-centred or claim to be wiser

than others. Also, he must not be hot tempered. He must be ready to die for his people and keep intact the confidence reposed in him.

4.5   Types of Leadership

The following are types of leadership:

(a)   **Traditional leadership**

Traditional leadership is hereditary. It is achieved or attained through inheritance and traditional honours e.g. chieftaincy titles to worthy indigenes who have contributed meaningfully to the growth of the community.

(b)   **Religious leadership**

This is achieved through divine call. Religious leaders throughout the world claim that they received divine call at one time or the other of life to carry out certain divine instruction(s) in the service of God. Such leadership is found in all religious sects.

(c)   **Political leadership**

Political leadership is attained through participation in politics and belonging to a political party. Examples of such leadership in a democratic setting include the posts of head of state (President), Governor, Chairman, Ministers and so on. Also, at the levels of trade unionism, student unionism e.t.c, political leadership can also emerge.

(d)   Community leadership

This is attained through competence, hardworking and dedication to the community affairs. Also, it could be attained through philanthropic activities and the amount of interest shown to the progress of the community as a whole.

4.6   Qualities of a Followership

a.   He or she must be loyal to the leadership

b.   He or she must be highly disciplined

c.   He or she must not engage in anything that can tarnish the reputation of the leadership

d.   He must believe in hard work as a means of ascending to greatness.

e.   He must be dutiful and conscientious

f.   He must cooperate with other members of the community

g.   He must look up to leaders for order, protection and progress

CHAPTER FIVE: GOVERNMENT

In every human society, people recognize the need for rules and regulations, orderliness, obedience to the societal laws, norms, values and cooperation. For these essential ingredients of a functional society to be put in place, a machinery known as government has to be established. The term government is very wide. For example, it consists of all members of the society. Though, there are certain individuals entrusted and authorized to run the government but these individuals were elected by members of the society through the process of election. When we talk of elected government in this respect, we mean a democratically elected one as in liberal democracy.

Government can therefore be defined as machinery put in place by the people of a nation to administer, coordinate, regulate and to oversee their affairs. This definition is applicable to a democratic government. That is, a government that emerged in line with the constitution of the country where it emerged. Government may emerged by means of force e.g. totalitarianism and autocratic governments. In whichever form a government emerged, one basic thing is that, its primary duty is to control the activities and behaviour of men and maintain a well ordered society.

Government is a necessary social institution not only because every human being is a political animal, but also because of the need to control the activities and behaviour of men, equal distribution of resources (natural and manmade) and to institutionalize arrangement under which the resources available within a particular geographical area could be shared and or utilized for the good of all the people within such area.

To ensure a functional society and guide against extinction, there is need to evolve an organ to resolve conflicts in a binding manner, defend the society against external attack or from being absorbed by another society, protect lives and properties of all members of the society etc. The societal organ charged with the performance of these functions is called government.

5.1 Forms and Systems of Government

There are many forms and systems of government. The form of government operated by any state is the standard identification mark of such a state. For example, we say a state is socialist, capitalist, democratic, autocratic etc, depending on the system of government being used in that state. It may be difficult to pin down the government of a state to a particular label; this is because forms of government tend to overlap. One basic thing is that people tend to see their forms of government as unique, different or better than others, they see it having some advantages which others do not have. That is why people are ready to shed the last drop of their blood to fight the course of their government, especially where the people religiously have faith in their form of government.

Certain factors determine the type of government a particular state will operate. These include history, population, geography, economy, social structure, religion, political, culture and social forces.

5.2 Systems of Government

The world systems of government include liberal democracy, monarchy, aristocracy, oligarchy, autocracy and totalitarianism.

(a) Liberal democracy

This is government of the people by the people and for the people. It is the type of government in which some individual. Politicians are empowered to serve the interest of their people in government. It is a system of government that is masses oriented, in that all eligible adults are entitled to participate in the process of electing those to rule them. In liberal democracy, the vote of every individual is his power.

Characteristics of Liberal Democracy

i. In a liberal democratic system of government, there is usually more than one political party competing for power.

ii. The competition for power is based on established form of standard or procedure.

iii. Pressure groups e.g. labour union, student union and other voluntary organizations are not subject to close control by government, this is to enable them check extreme action of government.

iv. The mass media c.g. radio, television, newspapers enjoy some degree of independence and freedom from government control.

v. The representative assembly e.g. legislature, has some form of control over the executive but the judiciary is independent of both the legislative an executive

All the above characteristics exist under normal situation. There are some circumstances that could make the government to act contrary to any of the characteristics. For example, government may decide to close down any media house that is fond of reporting negative news or fallacious information against the government. Also, when a state of emergency is declared in a country or state, some of these freedoms are suspended or curtailed.

(b)   **Monarchical system of government**

Monarchy is basically a kind of government by one person, usually the King or Queen. Monarchy is the oldest system of government. Ascendance to the throne of this government is hereditary. For example, only the son of a King or Queen or somebody from his/her lineage can become head of government. In this system of government, there are no legal limitations to the powers of the monarch and the monarch may not be accountable to his subjects as regards his stewardship. It is a dynastic system of rule in which the status is transferred from parents to children and from generation to generation.

Hereditary monarchical type is still in operation in places like Britain, Saudi Arabia, Morocco, Sweden, etc up till date.

(c) **Aristocracy**

This is government by a few rich people in the society. This few rich people, because of their high status, power and wealth has political power. The privileged positions of the aristocrats place great emphasis on virtue, morals and intellectual superiority. It is a kind of position that can only be ascribed nor achieved. It is a kind of government that perpetuates itself by passing the privilege from generation to generation.

(d) **Oligarchy**

This is government by a minority of the society. It is made up of people whose sole asset in the society is political power. This minority people monopolise political power. Variants of oligarchy are authoritarianism and totalitarianism. Other systems of government may harbour authoritarianism and totalitarianism characteristics', depending on the degree of degeneracy

(e)   **Autocracy**

This is government by self-proclaimed leader or a leader who has imposed himself over the people. This type of leader used to be high handed in dealing with people. Such leaders do not rely on elections to get to power and where they passed through elections, such elections are always rigged to make sure they remain in power whether the people want them in power or not. Military government is an example of such government, in most cases such government is not only illegal but also contradicts the constitutional provision of the state as to the laid down rules for ascending the political throne or assuming leadership position in the state.

(f)   **Totalitarianism**

This is government in which the leader makes use of force to secure obedience among members. It is the type of government in which there is an official ideology to be perpetuated. Unlike liberal democracy, the government monopolises the mass media. Also, private associations are largely controlled by government, the principle of separation of power is highly discouraged and political power is monopolized by one political party.

5.3   Forms of Government

This simply means the various ways by which government is organized in order to maintain stability and political order, also, to ensure peaceful co-existence in the society. These include federalism unitary, confederacy, and communism and so on and so forth.

(a)   **Federalism**

This is a form of government in which governmental powers are shared between the three tiers of government, that is, federal, state and local government. Federalism is usually made up of states that were hitherto independent and autonomous, but agreed to come together and form a larger state and build up a central government by surrendering part of their power to the central government, and retaining part of it because of differences in identity.

(b) **Unitary government**

This is a form of government in which people were able to contain their ethnic or tribal differences and come under the rule of one central government. Ghana, Britain, Sierra-Leone, France and so on are examples of countries with unitary system of government.

(c) **Confederacy**

In this type of government, there is confederal arrangement between the various units or states that made up the government. Confederal arrangement in this sense, means right to break away. That is, any part of the state that has the ability to stand on its own can break away. Confederal arrangement was included in USSR federation. It was this that led to the breaking of USSR into many countries in 1995.

5.4 *Electoral process in Nigeria*

This is a political process or procedure. In a

democratic setting, the acceptable means of acquiring political position is by joining political party and by passing through an election. Electoral process therefore means the way and manner by which the people of a nation vote to elect their leaders or people to represent their interest in government.

First and foremost, it is the inauguration of the Electoral Commission. This is usually done by the government in power. The electoral commission is usually headed by Chairman at the national level. At the state level it is headed by the Commissioner. The Chairman is responsible for coordination of electoral activities at the national level, while at the state level the commissioner does.

Functions of the electoral commission include:
a. To register the voters and prepare the voters list for various elections.
b. Divide the nation into wards and constituencies
c. To register political parties
d. To register candidates for the election
e. To screen the candidates for the election
f. To fix the date and make preparation for the election

g. To recruit manpower for the election
h. To conduct election and declare election results
i. To audit the accounts of political parties.
j. To ensure that there is adequate security for the election.

Electoral Commission is expected to be autonomous or independent for the purpose of free and fair election. Examples of past and present electoral commissions in Nigeria include: Federal Electoral Commission (FEDECO), Nigeria Electoral Commission (NEC) and independent National Electoral Commission (INEC). Other important things about electoral process in Nigeria include:

Eligibility to Vote

(a)   **Age**: For any citizen of Nigeria to be eligible to vote in election he must have attained the age of 18 years.

(b)   **Resident**: He must have been residing in the area where he wants to vote or be voted for nothing less than one year before the election.

(c)   **Political office**: To be eligible to contest for any position/post in the nation politics, one must be a member of a registered political party and he must be elected by his party to do so. However, in recent years, an independent candidate who does not belong to any political party has been considered.

(d) **Registration**: Apart from being a citizen of Nigeria, every citizen is expected to register for the election. Anyone whose name is not found in the voter's register even though he is a Nigerian and of mature age to vote, will not be allowed to vote, because he has not satisfied voting requirement.

(e) **Election**: The dates of elections are fixed by the electoral commission. Representatives of all the parties are to be present at polling booth in addition to the neutral electoral supervisors/officers and other officers recruited by electoral commission to see to smooth conduct of the election.

(f) **Counting of voters cards**: After the election, the voter's cards are counted to know the winner(s).

(g) **Declaration of results/winners**: It is the duty of the Electoral Commission to declare the winners/ results especially the sensitive positions like that of president, Governors etc. Results at the level of Chairmanship/ Counsellorship may be announced by the State Electoral Commissioner if he is authorized by the Chairman to do so.

(h) **Challenging of results**

The election results may be challenged if the opponent has evidence to prove that the winner has rigged the election. And if the allegation has substantial evidence, the election may be nullified depending on the seriousness of the evidence and the electoral offence committed. Cases of electoral malpractices are handled by electoral tribunal.

All the processes discussed above are peculiar to direct election. Election may be indirect, for example, election of the President or Governor may not be done by the general public. It may be done by those elected by the people to represent them in the House of Assembly as was the case during the first republic.

CHAPTER SIX: THE ARMS OF GOVERNMENT

For the purpose of running an effective, efficient and purposeful government, that is free from over-concentration of power in the hands of a single individual which could lead to power intoxication and abuse of office, there are three arms of government in Nigeria. These include:

1.   The Executive
2.   The Legislative
3.   The Judiciary

6.1   The Executive

This is one of the essential organs of the government that is responsible for carrying out the functions of Head of State, President, Governor, Chairman etc. There are various types of executive, namely:

(a)   Single executive
(b)   Dual executive
(c)   Plural executive
(d)   Variant executive

(a)   **Single executive**: This is the type in which the

power of Head of State and Head of Government is conferred on a single person. In this situation, an individual functions as the Head of State and performs the Ceremonial functions.

(b)   **Dual executive**: This is the type in which the power of Head of State is vested on one person and the power of Head of government is conferred on another person. In this type of executive, there are two captains piloting the ship of the state. In essence, there are two heads, one is given the functions of the President and the second one is designated as the Prime Minister. The Prime Minister in this sense is the actual ruler of the state, he is the leader of government business, he formulates policies, appoints ministers, etc. While the President as the ceremonial head, receives visitors, signing treaties, bills and other international matters.

(c)   **The plural executive**: This is the type of executive in which more than two persons are allowed to perform leadership function in a state. There is usually a council headed by a Chairman chosen from members of the council on rotational basis. The Chairman has the last say in both national and international matters. This system of executive is usually operated where there is leadership problem, for example, where one ethnic group fears that another ethnic group may dominate the affairs of governance.

(d) **Variant executive**: This is the type in which executive carries out or performance the functions of all the arms of government. The principle of separation of power is not adhered to in this type of executive. Even when there is legislature, they only rubber stamp the executive actions.

6.2 Functions of Executive

The executive performs the following functions namely:

a. **Administrative functions:** The executive is the chief administrator of the state. He sees to the effective and efficient administration of the state. This is done through the various ministries under his control.

b. **Formulation and implementation of policies:** The executive formulates policies and implement them. He is the major decision maker in the state. Though, he takes the Interest of the people into consideration especially the powerful group in the society. The executive is able to take care of the people in his decisions because of his access to information.

c. **Financial function:** The executive is responsible for budgeting, allocation of money to the various segments of government. When such budget is made, it has to be sent to the house of assembly for approval before the executive could embark on any expenditure.

d. **Appointment function:** It is the function of the executive to appoint ministers, commissioners, advisers, ambassadors, etc. Before announcing the appointment to the general public, he must have lent it to the legislature for screening and approval. The legislature has the power to disapprove the appointment of any candidate that they feel is of questionable character or that does not merit such appointment.

e. **Ceremonial function:** The executive presides over all national ceremonies e.g. Independence day and so on and so forth.

f. **Legislative function:** The executive performs legislative function. He drafts bill and sends it to the legislature, and when this has been successfully passed, it returns back to executive for final assent. All other bills whether initiated by the legislature or the public must be assented by the executives after they must have been passed by the legislature.

g. **Diplomatic function:** The executive carries out negotiation with other states or countries on behalf of his country or state, sign treaties, trade agreement or bilateral agreement. When a diplomat is sent from another country it is the executive that receives his letter or credence.

h. **Security function:** The executive is the chief security officer of his state, he sees to the maintenance of laws and order through the

Police. The police are there to enforce the laws and see to it that whoever breaks the law is arrested and prosecuted. The warders are also there to keep in prison whoever has been sentenced by the law court.

i. **Emergency function:** When there is Emergency, it is the function of the executive to act immediately without any delay to save the situation. He may not need to obtain the approval of the house of assembly before taking action.

6.3   *The Legislative*

This is the law making arm of government. It consists of two house chambers namely, House of Representatives and house of senates. Members o house of representatives examine critically every bill that is sent to the house to determine its relevance, suitability and adaptability to the needs and yearnings of the people. And if it is a bill concerning regulation of behaviour of the people, they would ensure that the bill is not aimed at dehumanizing the people, that is, not against natural law. That is the reason why the legislative bodies are divided into committees e.g.

Committee on Education, Petroleum, Energy, Health etc.

When a bill has been successfully passed at the House of Representatives, it would now come to the Senate. The senate would go through the bill to determine its merits and to be satisfied that the bill was not hastily passed. Indeed, the senate is to check the excesses of the House of Representatives.

The legislative has some form of control over the executive but the judiciary is independent of both the executive and legislative arms.

6.4   Functions of Legislative

The legislative house performs the following functions:

1. **To make laws:** The bulk of the laws in the state are made by the legislature. In fact, their primary duty is to make good laws for the nation.

2. **Financial function:** The legislature performs financial function, in that they examine

thoroughly every budget sent to them by the executive to be sure that the budget is realistic. And that the proposed expenditure really worth it. In essence, the legislature is there to protect the interest of the masses being the middle people between the government and the governed. They would want to be sure that whatever budget made, takes good care of the welfare of the masses before approving it. They have power under the law to increase the amount budgeted by the executive or reduce it, though this has to be done in consultation with the executive.

3. **Appointment function:** The legislature performs appointment function. When executive nominates names for ministerial and ambassadorial posts, he has to send the list to the legislature for screening and approval. The legislature would now screen the candidates to be sure that they are suitable and qualified for the posts. The legislature has power to approve or disapprove the appointment of any candidate they considered unsuitable for the post.

4. **Budget monitoring:** The legislature performs the function of budget monitoring. This to be sure that the executive implements the approved budget accordingly. Where the executive deviates, the legislature has the power to call him to order.

5. **Judicial function:** The legislature performs judicial function; they settle disputes e.g. communal, labour and so on and so forth.

6. **Collegial function:** The legislature may be asked to elect the Governor or President as it was the case in the first republic. In such situation, only the legislative members would vote as against the situation under direct election whereby the masses elect the leaders through direct voting. Though the masses would still employ the legislature while the legislature would now vote to elect the executive. This type of election is called indirect election.

6.5 The Judiciary

This is the arm of government that is concerned with dispensation of justice. The judiciary is said to be the last hope of common man. And this arm is independent of both the executive and legislative. The judiciary is headed by the Attorney-General and Minister of Justice. It consists of the Judges and various courts of justice.

6.6   Functions of Judiciary

The functions performed by the judiciary include the following:

1. **Settlement of disputes:** The judiciary settles disputes between individual and another individual; individual and government, government and government etc. The judiciary settles disputes as prescribed by law.

2. **Interpretation of law:** The judiciary interprets the laws and determines its meaning when new problems and situations arise. This is necessary because if there is law and people do not understand it, it would be valueless and be of no use. In this regard it is the function of the judiciary to interpret the laws and give meaning to them.

3. **Protection of individual rights:** The judiciary

protects and defends individual's rights. Individual within the society has some rights that need be protected; these include the rights of movement, fair hearing, association, religion, freedom of speech etc. The judiciary protects these rights.

4. **Pronouncing judgment:** It is the function of the judiciary to pronounce judgment against the offender. After listening to the pros and cons of a case, the judiciary pronounces judgment against whoever is guilty and discharges and acquits whoever has been wrongly accused. Since an accused is presumed innocent until his case has been proved beyond all reasonable doubt.

5. **Advisory role to the government on legal matters:** The judiciary advises the government on legal implications of all governmental actions, may be towards the people at the national or international levels.

6. **Administering of oath of office:** The judiciary performs the function of administering oath of

office to newly

7. . During swearing in ceremony of new elected leaders, e.g. President, Governor, Chairman, Commissioners, Ministers etc the oath of office is usually administered by the judiciary.

6.7　Government and Mass Media

Mass media is the sole agent that acquaints the people with the activities of the government. In a democratic society, the government is set up by the people. That is, those who serve in government are elected by the people. The aim of the masses for electing people to serve them in government is usually to see that their interests are represented, protected and their welfare are accorded a priority.

Without adequate information in the society, there is likely to be communication gap that may result into misunderstanding, mistrust, suspicion and rebellion. That is why government and media are supposed to be partners in progress.

The various means of getting information include:

1. The radio
2. The television and
3. The newspapers.
4. Facebook
5. Twitter
6. You tube

The efforts of the government are made known to the people though the mass media. The mass media is given freedom to express its mind in a democratic government and also criticizes unpopular actions of the government. The mass media enables the citizens to understand their rights thereby saving them from embarrassment resulting from ignorance. In electing new leaders, the mass media have significant roles to play for example, campaigning is done through the mass media, information about the date of election, how to vote, when the voting would commence, the dos and don'ts in the polling booth as well as the results of the elections are made known through mass media.

In Nigeria, perhaps because of low level of enlightenment on the part of our leaders as a result of military interference and domination of politics, the role of the press had been misconstrued. Whenever the media criticized the government constructively in the past, journalists would be arrested and imprisoned. The situation had been such that all what government wanted was praises from the media not criticism, and this is contrary to the role of the mass media in a progressive society. Thus, any government that wants to succeed must handle the mass media as an important part of the government. In fact the mass media is the eye and mouth of the masses. If the mass media is allowed to do its work the way it should be done, it would bring about good governance.

CHAPTER SEVEN: CONCEPT OF RIGHTS

Rights according to Adefolarin (1981) are certain privileges that every citizen can enjoy in a country. Such rights are written in a constitution of every state. There are civil and political rights which a citizen can enjoy. The protections accorded these rights by the government are specified in the constitution.

Sheyin (1996) defined human rights as those privileges enjoyed by the citizens of a given state. These privileges are usually defined and enjoyed within (the bounds of the law) i.e. the law of the country. Sheyin stressed further that human rights are political privileges and civil liberties accruing to the citizens who are meant t be protected by the state. Any citizen who has any part of his rights infringed, can protest this in the law court for a redress.

Collin (1983) defined rights as the legal entitlements of every citizen in a state. In other words, rights are seen as the benefits the individual attracts from the state (Agagu, 1993). Rights are constitutional benefits of the citizens of a country which can be protested in the law court if violated by an individual or government. According to Agagu many philosophers contributed enormously to the development and refinement of the notion of rights.

Indeed, the history of rights and duties of a citizen can be traced back to the Greek philosophers. The French revolution of 1889 emerged with the declaration of the rights of man. As part of the declaration, the Revolution asserted that men are born free and equal and therefore should remain as such. They stressed that the natural rights of men are liberty, property, security and resistance to oppression (Agagu, 1993).

In summary, rights can be defined as the privilege or benefits accruing to man for belonging to a particular state. Rights are legal in that they are contained in the constitution of the state and some of the rights are peculiar or exclusively reserved for the citizens of a particular state. For example, not all the human rights contained in Nigerian constitution can be extended to foreigners living in Nigeria, likewise not all human rights accruable to Briton are extended to foreigners especially those that have to do with political and economic.

7.1 Fundamental Human Rights

The Nigerian independence constitution of 1960 made detailed provisions for fundamental human rights. Also Chapter IV of both the 1979 and 1985 constitutions of the Federal Republic of Nigeria contain the fundamental human rights of Nigeria citizens. These rights include:

(a) Right to live

(b) Right to dignity of human person

(c) Right to personal liberty

(d) Right to fair hearing

(e) Right to private and family life

(f) Right to freedom of thoughts, conscience and religion

(g) Right to freedom of expression and the press

(h) Right to peaceful assembly and association

(i) Right to freedom of movement

(j) Right to freedom from discrimination

(k) Right to own property

(a) **Right to life:** This may be said to be the most important of all the human rights. Everyone has right to live and no one has right to terminate life of another person except when one is found guilty of an offence that carries death penalty by the law court. Offences like armed robbery, treasonable felony, aborted coup d'état, etc could warrant death penalty if anyone is found guilty of them by the law court.

(b) **Right to dignity of human person:** A person should not be subjected to any form of torture or degrading treatment that is capable of dehumanizing him. Every person has right to good reputation, good name and any defamation of character could be protested in the law court for a redress.

(c) **Right to personal liberty:** Personal liberty is an entitlement of every citizen. No one has right to interfere with or deprive any citizen of his liberty.

(d) **Right to fair hearing:** Every citizen has right to fair hearing in the law court, no matter the allegation levelled against him. This is necessary because an accused is presumed innocent until his case has been proved beyond all reasonable doubt. Thus, the court has to grant reasonable time to everyone accused of one misdemeanour or the other to defend himself before judgment.

(e) **Right to private family life:** Individual citizen is entitled to privacy of his life, home, telephone correspondence, telegraphic and conversations. He has right to marry and rear children. A couple could decide to manage their family affairs the way it pleases them provided they do not contradict the law of the state without any external interference.

(f) **Right to freedom of thought, conscience and religion:** Every individual has the right to think the way he feels appropriate to him. He is free for his conscience and to worship whatever he considers appropriate to him. No one has the right to impose his religion on another person or discriminate against someone because of his different religious belief. In fact, Nigeria is a secular state; no religion is a state-one.

(g) **Right to freedom of expression and the press:**

Every individual is free to express his opinion about any national issue. No one should be punished for expressing his opinion over the radio, television or newspaper on any matter.

(h) **Right to peaceful assembly and association:** Every citizen has right to join any peaceful assembly or any association of his choice without any fear or harassment or embarrassment from any one.

(i) **Right to freedom of movement:** Every individual is free to move to, and live in any part of Nigeria without any discrimination. No one has right to deprive any Nigerian from coming into Nigeria or deport any Nigerian from Nigeria.

(j) **Right to freedom from discrimination:** Every Nigerian citizen is free from being discriminated against in any part of Nigeria may be as a result of tribe, state or sex.

(k) **Right to own property:** As a citizen, one is free to work and own properties. No one has right to seize the property of another citizen or convert the property of another citizen to his own. Even when government acquires land that belongs to a private individual, he would need to pay the person compensation that is commensurable to the value of the land.

As good as the rights are, it is important to stress that they have limitations. The citizens need to be enlightened so as to know their limit and guide against overdoing things, as one may land himself or herself in trouble for wrong behaviour. For example, the constitution says everyone has the right to life no one should terminate life of another person. But when you terminate somebody's life, it is obvious that your life must be terminated after the court must have found you guilty.

You have right to express your opinion or publish your opinion on any national issue but not to the extent of publishing false allegation that cannot be substantiated against the government or an individual if this is done, one may be arrested or prosecuted.

Your right to own properties do not extent to embezzling government money or public fund to acquire properties. When anyone tries this, his properties may be seized and forfeited to the government in addition to being jailed.

You have right to join peaceful assembly or any association of your choice. But any assembly that turns violent or tends to cause destruction of lives and properties, may be stopped by the Police may even decide not to allow such assembly to hold.

Based on the above, it is right to say that every individual is the chief protector of his rights, if you want to enjoy your rights, you must respect the rights of others. Because the moment you infringed on the right of another person, you have committed an offence against the state, not that person alone, and the state would handle you through the law enforcement agents and take you up for prosecution. During the process of investigation, you may be rough handled if the law enforcement agents are not convinced of your innocence of the case or If they feel that you are likely to make confession that would be helpful to them to discover other criminals. Also, if they feel that you have not confessed.

In essence, you only retain all your rights when you have not committed an offence or be implicated in a criminal offence. The moment any of these happens you may not enjoy some of your rights until may be you are found innocent, discharged and acquitted.

7.2 Obligations

Just like the citizens of a state possess certain undeniable right they also owe the state certain responsibilities and duties which they must perform as citizens to keep the government in existence. The government also has certain responsibilities and functions which it must perform to the citizens on behalf of the state. All these are obligations. Obligations therefore refer to civil or social actions of the citizens which directly or indirectly contribute to effective government. It has to do with the expectations of the citizens to the government.

Thus, it is wrong of any person or group of persons to always talk of their rights from the government without talking of their obligations to the government, both are very important for the development of human society. For example, it is the rights of every citizens to attend good school, to enjoy good health and drink pipe bone water, but also as a citizen, you need to pay your tax regularly to enable government get money for providing the amenities. Anyone who denies government of his obligations is not clean to challenge government of not protecting his or her rights.

7.3 Responsibilities and Duties of Nigerian Citizens

According to the 1989 Constitution of the Federal Republic of Nigeria, the Nigerian citizens owe the following duties and responsibilities to perform to the state:

(a) To abide by the constitution, respect its ideals and institutions, the national flag, the national anthem, the national pledge and legitimate and properly constituted authorities.

(b) To protect and preserve public property, and fight against misappropriation and squandering of public funds.

(c) To help enhance the power, prestige and good name of the country and to defend the country and render national service as may be required.

(d) To respect the dignity and religion of other citizens and the rights and the legitimate interest of others, and to live in unity and harmony and in the spirit of common brotherhood.

(e) To make positive and useful contributions to the advancement, progress and well-being of the community where he resides.

(f) To work conscientiously in his lawful and chosen occupation and to abstain from any activity detrimental to the general welfare of other citizens or to the country.

(g) To ensure proper upbringing of his children

(h) To participate in and defend all democratic processes and practices.

(i) To render assistance to appropriate and lawful agencies in the maintenance of law and order.

(j) To declare his income honestly to appropriate and lawful agencies and to pay his tax promptly.

7.4 *Responsibilities and Duties of Nigerian Government*

The Nigerian Constitution of 1979 spells out the responsibilities and duties expected of authorities and persons exercising legislative, executive or judicial powers. These include the following:

(a) Protection of life and property. The right to life and properly must be guaranteed by the government. Every citizen must be protected.

(b) To exploit the natural resources available within the geographical zone and to enhance the quality of life of the citizens.

(c) To defend the sovereignty of the nation and save the country from external attack. Also, to negotiate political, cultural and economic relations with other nations.

(d) To render essential services such as provision of water, good health services, construction of roads, etc. to the people.

(e) To ensure equal distribution of income, reduces unemployment and caters for the general welfare of the citizens.

(f) To settle disputes and reconcile conflicts in any part of the state.

(g) To provide laws that would ensure better life for the citizens and make the society to be orderly.

(h) To enforce order within the state

(i) To embark on policies that will be of innumerable benefit to the entire people. That is, masses oriented programmes, and

(j) To ensure accountability and probity in the day-to-day running of affairs of the people.

CHAPTER EIGHT: NATIONAL ETHICS AND DISCIPLINE IN NATIONAL LIFE

8.1 Conceptualizing Ethics

In any society or institution, there must be rules and regulations that guide the behaviour of the people. This is necessary because there are societal goals or institutional goals which every society or institution aims at achieving, and for the purpose of effective and efficient realization of these goals, there is need to put some rules in place that would tailor the behaviour of the people towards achieving the goals. Since any contrary behaviour on the part of any member of the society or institution could jeopardize the achievement of these goals. These rules are ethics. It is the guiding moral principle or code of conduct of an institution, profession, or society.

Ethics are not the same as moral. If one lacks moral we may say he is immoral or morally bankrupt or deficient. Ethics are the rules of authoritative standard or the rules that set the right and wrong conducts while morality is a pattern of behaviour.

In this regard, for members of the society to be acceptable they must comply with the ethics of that society. The society would out-rightly reject those that do not conform to the standard rules of conduct and such people are called non-conformists. In every society we have non-conformists and another group called deviants. Deviants are the people who deviate from the societal norms or values and these sorts of people are usually sanctioned or punished by the society.

Ethics are necessary in every society to ensure the continuity of the society and guide against behaviour or actions that could extinct the society. Ethics are not peculiar to the state alone, also they are found in various professions e.g. medical, law, teaching and so on and so forth.

8.2 Conceptualizing Discipline

Discipline may be defined as the ability to control oneself by conforming to the societal rules and regulations. Discipline is a necessary ingredient for societal development, growth and stability. A disciplined society is one in which the members cultivate the habit of obedience to the rules or ethics of that society. When there is discipline in a society, there would be peace, and peace is an indispensable pre-requisite to economic growth and prosperity.

To make a child become a disciplined adult, the journey starts from childhood. The initial training of a child's mind begins with the parent and older members of the family e.g. brother and sister. When the child has grown up, the issue of inculcation of discipline becomes an affair of the school, the church/mosque, the peer group, etc. All these bodies are referred to as agents of socialization.

Socialization is a process of inculcating the norms and values of the society in the young ones in order to make them useful and reliable members of the society. When a child internalizes the norms and values of the society, he would not only be useful to himself but the society as whole. An undisciplined person is one who is in the habit of contravening the rules or ethics of the society. He is a person whose behaviour or actions are capable of jeopardizing the achievement of the societal or institutional goals. Indiscipline is the mother of social vices that are capable of hampering the well-being of a society.

The case of indiscipline is a notorious one in Nigeria today, as observed by Oyeneye (1997), the rate of indiscipline has reached an alarming proportion that children no longer respect their teachers or even parents. Among the adults, the level of indiscipline cannot be quantified. People no longer comply with the norms and values of the society because everybody wants to make it by all means.

The love of money has eroded the traditional norms and values. In addition to the love of money is the over enthusiasm for foreign culture at the expense of traditional one. Other factors that breeds indiscipline in Nigerian society are bad leadership, military intervention in politics, inadequate attention to Citizenship Education as a subject in Nigerian schools, failure to professionalized teaching, poor condition of service of Nigerian teachers, excessive respect for rich without finding out the root of their money and so on and so forth.

8.3 Some Indisciplinary Acts in Nigerian Society

In Nigeria today, these are some of indisciplinary acts:

(1)   Armed robbery

(2)   Bunkery

(3)   Embezzlement of public fund

(4)   Ritual killing

(5)   Forgery

(6)   Examination malpractices

(7)   Rigging of election

(8)   Thuggery

(9)   Lack of respect for elders

(10)   Leaking of official secrets

(11)   Sexual harassment

(12)   Advance "fee" fraud (419)

(13)   Placing one interest above national interest

(14)   Bribery and corruption

(15)   Tribalism, favouritisms or ethnicity

(16)   Lack of respect for constituted authority

(17)   Lateness to work or absenteeism

(18)   Reckless driving or failure to observe traffic rules

(19)   Inflation of contract fees

(20)   Inflation of prices of goods

(21)   Hoarding of goods

(22)   Accusing someone falsely

(23)   Breaking or damaging of government property

(24)   Harbouring a criminal

(25) Aiding and abetting

(26) Stealing

(27) Lying

(28) Bearing false witness

(29) Laziness

(30) Drinking while drunk

(31) Breaking traffic rules

(32) Selling adulterated drugs

(33) Smuggling

(34) Cheating

(35) Vandalism

(36) Raping

(37) Cultism to mention a few.

8.4 *Public Control of Indiscipline*

In the past, various efforts have been made by the Nigerian government to instil discipline in Nigerians. Some of the measures taken included the launching of War against Indiscipline (WAI), institution of Code of Conduct Bureau, War Against Indiscipline and corruption (WAIC), introduction of National Youth Service Corps (NYSC) to reduce ethnicity, introduction of corrupt practised investigation tribunal introduction of public complaint commission, introduction of Mass Mobilization for Self-Reliance and Economic Recovery (MAMSER) and National Rebirth.

All these measures introduced by government to control indiscipline achieved little or nothing because those who introduced them did not lead by example. Some of them committed atrocities that are worse than those committed by ordinary Nigerians. For example, some of them looted the treasury and transferred billions of Naira into foreign banks while some introduced the use of various means to kill their critics e.g. letter bomb, poison, gun to mention a few. And if the leaders are not discipline what do you expect of the followers.

CHAPTER NINE: NATIONAL IDENTITY

In order to identify a group of people, they must have something in common. At the family level, people bear the same surname as a mark of identity. In extended family system, people are bound together by facial or body marks. The national level is not an exemption, there are certain things which bind the people of a nation together, these things are referred to as National Identity. National Identity simply means absolute sameness or exact likeness. Every citizen of a nation, no matter the tribe, state or local government of origin shares from these things. In essence, these are things that bind us together as a nation or people.

9.1 National Symbols

These are signs or objects that show the identity of the nation and stress togetherness. These include:

(1) National currency

(2) National flag

(3) National anthem

(4) National pledge

(5) Coat of arms

(6) Historical symbols

(7) National heroes and heroines

(8) The Nigerian passport and so on and so forth.

People respect these symbols because they bind the people together.

(a) **National Currency:** This is the nation's legal tender which is generally acceptable as means of settling debt for all commercial transactions. It is issued by the Central Bank of Nigeria in various denominations. These includes: I Kobo, 50 Kobo, One Naira, and Two Naira in coins form. In Naira notes we have #5, #10, #20, #50, #100, #200, #500 ad #1,000. Only the Central Bank of Nigeria is authorized to print money in Nigeria. It is an offence for anyone who refuses to collect Nigerian money for settlement of debt once it carries the Central Bank number.

(b) **National Flag:** The Nigerian national flag was designed by Mr. Taiwo Akinkunmi in 1959. The flag was made public for the first time on October 1, 1960, the day Nigeria obtained her political independence from the British government. The flag consists of three main parts namely, green white green colours. The green colour symbolizes the green farmlands and forest from which the nation's agriculture wealth is derived and where majority of Nigerians are employed, while the white colour symbolizes peace and unity.

(c)   **The National Anthem:** The nation's national anthem is a song that is sang to inculcate a kind of patriotism an respect to the nation in the citizens. It is obligatory for everybody to stand at attention when this song is on. This song is sang in school every morning and before the commencement of any important government programme at the local, state and federal level, the song must be sang.

(d)   **The National Pledge:** The nation's national pledge is a kind of commitment on the part of every citizen to be loyal, honest and be dedicated to the cause of the nation. It is a call to serve, to be responsible and participate in making the nation great. It is a saying that is expected to be translated into action.

(e)   **Coat of arms:** Nigerian coat of arms is a

symbol used to represent the sovereignty of the nation. It represents the unity, authority and power of the country. It is made up of an eagle which is mounted on a black shield. The black shield represents the good soil of Nigeria; the eagle represents the strength of Nigeria while the horses represent the dignity and pride of Nigeria. The mark on the shield which looks letter "Y" represents the River Niger and Benue which flow from parts of Nigeria. The flower stands for the beauty of Nigeria. The Nigeria's motto: Unity and Faith is written on the coat of arms.

(f)   **Historical Symbols:** This has to do with those objects used to mark important events that occurred in the history of a nation or to immortalize names of some important people who had made significant roles in the development of their country. In Nigeria, these include status of the unknown soldiers in Abuja, formerly in Lagos, Emotan in Binin-Clty, Oranmiyan's staff at lle-lfe etc.

(g)   **National Heroes and Heroines:** Heroes and heroines are male and female Nigerians who had contributed immensely to the political, social and economic development of Nigeria. They are people who have served the nation at various levels in the past and had rendered a meritorious service to the nation. Such people in Nigeria Include: Moremi of Ife, Queen Amina of Zaria, Alhaji (Sir) Abubakar Tafawa Balewa, Sir Ahmadu Bello, Chief M.K.O Abiola, Chief Obafemi Awolowo, Alvan Ikoku etc. Several efforts have been made by respective governments to immortalize these people. These include naming street, buildings, and schools after these great Nigerians. Examples of these are Moshood Abiola Polytechnics, Abeokuta; Obafemi Awolowo University, lle-Ife; Alvan Ikoku College of Education; Michael Otedola College of Primary Education, Epe; to mention a few.

(h)   **The Nigerian Passport:** This is an official symbol. It is a document issued to the citizens by the federal government of Nigeria for the purpose of identification when travelling abroad. The passport is purely issued to identify and to prove nationality.

9.2 Culture

Culture may be defined as the way of life of people. It is the total way of life of people which includes their belief, way of dressing way of building houses, marriages, festivals and languages which they share and transmit from generation to generation. Culture has two broad areas namely: materials culture and immaterial culture. Material culture refers to materials like arts and crafts, foods, houses, dresses, artefacts, tools as well as the technology of a people. Non-material culture refers to the norms, values, beliefs or religion, language, ideas and philosophy, music and dance, drama, festivals, ceremonies folklores and so on and so forth. Both material and immaterial culture influences each other.

In Nigeria, there are about 250 ethnic groups and 450 dialects. The three major ones consist of about 58% of the entire population of Nigeria and these are Hausa, Yoruba and Igbo (Adegoke, 1996). The following aspects of Nigerian culture will be considered:

(a)   **Language:** In Nigeria, we have many languages. For example, we have Yoruba, Igbo, Hausa Efik, Ilaje, Ikale and so on and so forth..

(b)   **Festivals:** In Nigerian society, festivals are many and very according to different cultural groups. In Yoruba society, we have Agemo, Oro, Eyo and Egungun festivals. While in Hausaland we have Argugu fishing festival, Pategi regatta. Edo people have the Ugieerhoba festival, the igbo have Offalo and new yam festivals, Odu festival is found among the Ijaws of Delta and Rivers State. Eje festival among the Ikale of Ondo state.

(c)   **Religion:** The three main religions in Nigeria are Christianity, Islam and traditional religion (paganism).

(d)   **Art and Crafts:** Nigeria is well known throughout the world for her arts and crafts. These include metal work, wood work and leather work. Some towns in Nigeria are well known for one art and craft or the other. For example, Kano is well known for leather work; Ife and Ilorin for pottery, brass; Porthacourt, Opobo and Epe are famous for boat building; Bida, Benin and Kano are well known for brass work; Abeokuta, Ibadan and Ijebu-Ode are famous for Indigo-Dyed cloth and so on and so forth.

(e) **Music:** There are various traditional music in Nigeria. Music brings happiness and joy to the people. In most cases, Nigerians have different music for different occasions. For example, the music for burial ceremony is different from that of naming ceremony or marriage. Some of the traditional music in Nigeria include: Apala, Sakara, Juju among the Yoruba: Npogid and Atilogwu among the lgbo; Gogo among the Hausa and Biripo among the Ikale of Ondo State.

(f) **Marriage Ceremony:** Every tribe in Nigeria has a way of conducting its marriage traditionally. One important thing that cuts across all the tribes is the idea of combining traditional marriage with modern day marriage contracted in the court, church or mosque, even when the traditional items being collected for marriage would still be collected by the bride's family.

9.3 Ways by Which Government Can Encourage Cultural Development in Nigeria

Culture as a way of life of the people can be promoted and encouraged through the following ways:

(a) By inculcating culture in the curriculum of our schools. In this respect, culture would be taught in schools as a subject.

(b) By documenting our cultural ways of life in video films, television and radio for the next generation.

(c) By building monument or cultural centre in each local government area where people could see the ancient remains and various cultural ways of the previous generations.

(d) By celebrating cultural festivals annually at the national level

(e) By budgeting a substantial amount of money every year for the promotion and development of culture both at the federal, state and local government levels.

(f) By monitoring the activities of our radio and

television stations to ensure that they adapt their programmes to the local needs of the people.

(g) By encouraging tourism and movement within Nigeria.

(h) By establishing an enlightenment campaign department in the Ministry of Youths and Culture that would be charged with the duty of enlightening the populace on the need to preserve and perpetuate their culture. And that any nation who gives up her culture completely at the expense of another culture would be termed a "cultural rebel".

CHAPTER TEN: NIGERIAN ENVIRONMENT

Man's environment simply means the abode of man and things that surround him. The things that surround man can be categorized into two namely, natural and man-made things. Man's environment can also be classified into two namely, physical and social environment.

Physical environment consists of soils, vegetation, landforms, water, natural resources like climate, minerals etc. Social environment on the other hand, can be described as a situation whereby two or more people live and interact with each other and sharing the common opinion and thus, developing a culture. Social environment could be said to include a small group of people, town, village, state, nation or country. etc. Man is a social animal, as a result of this, man enjoy living in company of another or other people.

Both the physical and social environments influence man, at the same time, man influences his environment. The environmental influence on man is felt in the areas of dressing, types of house, types of occupation, foods, construction etc while man's influence on the environment is concerned with adaptation of the environment to man's need. For example, man's activities on the environment includes, building of houses, construction of roads, dams, fashioning of tools and invention of cars, airplanes, train and exploitation of natural resources which are available in the environment.

Nigerian environment is made up of rural environment and urban environment.

1.   **Rural environment**

This is made up of village settlements and it is where about 80% of the population of the country engage in agriculture. There is general absence of social amenities like pipe borne water, electricity, good roads, hospitals etc in most rural environment in Nigeria. The situation is one of little or no development. For example, farming methods and housing situation remains as primitive as they were in pre-colonial days. That explains why people move to the urban cities so as to enjoy the amenities and the opportunities.

2.   **Urban environment**

This comprises of towns and cities like Ibadan, Lagos, Akure, Benin-City, Okitipupa, lrele, Kaduna, Abuja etc. In most urban cities in Nigeria there are robberies, theft etc. Though the basic social amenities are provided but they are not enough for use of the teaming population. In spite of these problems, people still move to urban centres, this is as a result of job opportunities and anticipated good condition of living.

10.1 *Exploration and Exploitation of the Environment*

Through exploration, a lot of facts have emerged about the environment. It has been discovered that the Nigerian environment consists of many elements such as underlying rocks, weathered debris, land forms, soil, vegetation, mountain/hills, animals and water etc. Nigeria is also endowed with abundant natural resources some of which are already being exploited by the government and some which are yet to be exploited. Some of these natural content of Nigerian environment have been exploited and used for man's needs e.g. food, fibre, generation of energy, living space, recreation, transportation and other things useful to man's existence. As the population increases, the demand for these resources increased. In Nigeria, there is problem of environmental degradation. Environmental degradation is a process of subjecting the land, plants and animals to mass destruction, infertility or danger through the activities of man or natural phenomenon.

10.2 Environmental Degradation Problems

These are various activities that degrade the environment.

a) Pollution: This refers to contamination of the environment by foreign or alien properties that adversely affect the lives and livelihood of human beings.

b) Deforestation (cutting of trees indiscriminately without replacement). The three types of pollution are air, land and water pollution

c) Erosion

d) Drought

e) Flooding

f) Releasing of poisonous toxic into the air

g) Continuous farming on a parcel of land without allowing it to fallow or regain its fertility

h) Uncontrolled dumping of refuse on the environment

i) Noise

j) Oil spillage

k) Bush burning

10.3 Effects of Pollution

(a) Air pollution can reduce the purity of the air breath-in by man

(b) Pollution can lead to lung disease.

(c) Noise pollution can lead to disturbances and ill-health,

(d) Water pollution can cause diseases like water blindness in man

(e) Pollution can lead to increase infant mortality rate.

(f) Water pollution can lead to the death of aquatic animals e.g. fish frogs etc.

10.4 Solution to the Problems of Pollution

1) People should be enlightened on the need to boil water before drinking it.

2) People should maintain good sanitation habit.

3) Waste materials should be referred to incinerator for burning.

4) Government should ensure that all landlords provide latrine/ toilet in their houses.

5) The amount of pollution by industries should be regulated

6) Government should try as much as possible to provide portable water for both the rural and urban populace especially those in oil producing areas where the problem of oil spillage occurs constantly.

7) Government should enact a law, making bush burning an offence punishable under the law. This is because bush burning can lead to untimely destruction of plants and animals

8) People should be encouraged to plant trees to replace those being cut for man's use.

9) Usefulness of the environment to man should be taught in schools.

10.5 National and International Conservation Agencies

There has been campaign at both the national and international levels on the need to conserve or preserve our environment. This is necessary in view of the importance of environment to both plants and animals. For example, the trees planted at the surrounding of our houses serve many useful purposes for man as well as for birds of the air. Plants produce oxygen which is needed for man. During hot season, trees by the sides of the house reduce the rate of heat on the house. Also, our herbs and traditional medicines are made from the trees. Animals in the bush also have their importance to man, they produce waste that helps the fertility of the soil. If all animals are destroyed or killed through hunting activities a time may come when there would be no bush animals. Indiscriminate cutting and burning of the bush would lead to a situation whereby some important trees and leaves needed for herbal healing of man would no longer be available. If all the trees are cut down, birds of the air would have difficulty of where to rest.

Some of the national agencies charged with the responsibility of enlightening man on the need for environmental conservation include:

(a)   Federal Environmental Protection Agency (FEPA)

(b)   Nigerian Conservation Foundation (NCF) which is a private organization being funded by Chevron.

(c)   Nigerian Environmental Study Team (NEST)

etc.

These agencies have been studying and providing solutions to Nigerians environmental problems. Also, there are departments of environmental studies in some Nigerian universities e.g. Lagos State University (LASU). The purpose of this is to enlighten and train agents for conservation of environment.

At the international level, some of the agencies commissioned by the world bodies to monitor and educate the world on the state of the global environment include:

1. United Nations Development Programme (UNDP)

2. United Nations Global Environmental Monitoring Systems (UNGEMS)

3. Environmental Sound Management of Inland Waters (ESMOIW)

4. Global Assembly of Land Degradation (GALD)

5. Friend of the Earth (FOE) etc.

10.6   Other Useful Readings

10.7 The Obstacles Obstructing Citizenship Education from Achieving the National Objectives

Introduction

Introduction of a new policy is not as desirable as the achievement of the objectives of the policy. Nigerian government is noted for formulation of good policies that are capable of taking the nation to Eldorado, in the realm of social, political, economic, physical and spiritual development. But the problem lies with the implementation which is most cases negate or jeopardize the achievement of the objectives of the policies. When a policy fails to achieve the pre-stated objectives or goals, the efforts put to the implementation of the policy vis-a-vIs the financial resources, may be said to be a colossal waste. Many attractive educational policies put in place failed to achieve their real objectives, due to what seems like lack of commitment on the part of the government to give the policies a down to earth attention that are pre-requisite to the achievement of success of the policies.

The same is the introduction of Citizenship Education into the curriculum of schools in Nigeria which may be said to be a fiasco due to the magnitude of criminality and the rate at which most Nigerians commit crimes both at home and abroad.

The introduction of Citizenship Education into the curriculum of Nigerian schools was another giant step taken by the government to prepare the citizens not only to be useful to them but to contribute meaningfully to the socio-economic, political and peaceful co-existence of the society. But it is unfortunate that Nigeria, even with over 158 years of formal education, and with almost 55 years of political independence, the country is still infested according to Oyeneye (1996), with a high level of indiscipline especially among the so-called educated elite.

It is doubtful if the course Citizenship Education has actually achieved its objectives of being in the curriculum of Nigerian schools, this is evident in the large scale commission of crimes going on within the country. The level of lawlessness among Nigerians today, calls for serious attention. Indiscipline manifests at all strata of the nation's life. Students are no longer ready to study before they pass their examinations, drivers are no longer ready to obey traffic rules, those at the helm of the nation's affairs no longer respect the rules of the law, and people are enslaved in the bondage of poverty despite the abundant natural resources of the nation. People want to make it through short-cut by engaging in in-human behaviours like advanced fee fraud, popularly known as 419, armed robbery, pen robbery, ritual killings, selling of human parts for charms, religious riots, prostitution human trafficking, embezzlement of public funds, political killings, terrorism to mention a few.

The level of ignorance among the people is of alarming proportion. For example, how do you account for mass termination of people's lives because of trivial issues like: he insulted my God, prophet or portray my religion in bad light? Is it the duty of man to fight for God or God to fight for man? If you insult my God, I would allow my God to fight you not me fighting you. When you fight for God, you are saying that God has no power to fight for himself. Ideally a living God is capable of fighting for himself, only a man-made god should be fought for by those who made it.

The focus of this paper therefore, is to examine the impediments on the way of Citizenship Education which have made it impossible for it to achieve its objectives.

Citizenship Education Conceptualized

Osakwe and Itedjere (1993), after acknowledging the difficulty in giving a precise definition of citizenship education, defined citizenship education as the systematic process through which young people acquire or internalize the values, sentiments and norms of the society in which they live and actively get involved to ensure that the common good of the citizens of the society is catered for including resisting anti-social and unguarded youthful exuberance. They explained citizenship education involves critical thinking, political activism or inquiry plus the goals and values of good citizens.

Ezegbe (1988) defines citizenship education as that education through which pupils in the school system will be taught about their rights, privileges, duties and responsibilities as good citizens and through which they will be encouraged to seek rights and privileges, performs their duties, and play a positive and active role in the society.

Coleman (1965) refers to citizenship education as political socialization. According to him, it is a process by which individuals acquire attitudes and feelings towards the political system and towards their role in it. He outlines what the process involves as:

- Learning how the political system works;

- The growth of feelings (positive and negative) about the systems and

- Development or non-development of a sense of competence to participate actively.

Going through all the above definitions, one thing is obvious and generally acceptable to all, is the fact that citizenship education is defined as training to become a good citizen who has been taught his civil rights and duties which include loyalty to the country, obedience to the laws of the state, the payment of national and local taxes and dues, and has learnt how to live and work together with other members of the society in a friendly and cooperative manner.

As Niemeyer (1957) rightly pointed out, "citizenship education is to help children to be socially sensitive, socially responsible and socially intelligent members of their community". Citizenship education finds its best application in the social context and so involves acquisition of knowledge, attitude and skills which the student utilizes for the overall benefit of the society (Nwanyanwu, 1977).

Asoga-Allen (2001), outlines certain qualities that must be found in anyone who has passed through citizenship education. These include:

- Being conscious of his rights and the rights of others;

- Being able to function effectively and efficiently in any governmental institution;

- Possession and demonstration of political knowledge;

- Being loyal and patriotic;

- Putting national interest above self-interest;

- Being highly disciplined;

- Interacting freely with the various ethnics groups in the country;

- Respecting the constitution of the Federal Republic of Nigeria;

- Being nationalistic in approach rather than tribalistic; and

- Making accountability and probity his watchword in both private and public lives.

In the light of the above, knowledge of citizenship education becomes inevitable for every citizen of a nation, not only to know their rights, duties and responsibilities to the government but also the duties and responsibilities of the government to the people. Also, the knowledge of the course would liberate every citizen from the bondage of ignorance, diseases, parochialism and make them live a useful life in the society.

The National Goals of Citizenship Education

Citizenship education was introduced to the curriculum of Nigerian schools to achieve the following national objectives:

1. To create the awareness of the Nigerian Constitution and the need for democracy in Nigeria.

2. To Introduce Nigerians to the functions and obligations of the government.

3. To make Nigerians fully aware of their rights and duties and to respect the rights of others.

4. To assist in the production of responsible, well-informed and self-reliant Nigerian citizens.

5. To inculcate the right values e.g. honesty, integrity, hard work, faithfulness, fairness and justice, to foster attitudes of togetherness, comradeship, cooperation and norms for the development of individual and Nigerian society.

6. To inculcate the concept of authority, leadership and followership into the citizens;

7.   To participate meaningfully in discussions on the Nigerian system of government and electoral process, arms of government, code of conduct for public officers and rules of mass media in national development.

8.   To articulate our history, national symbols, people and cultures of Nigeria; and

9.   To discuss the characteristic features of the Nigerian environment as well as the roles of national and international conservation agencies (Sheyin, 1996).

Problem Facing the Achievement of the Objective of Citizenship Education in Primary/Secondary School

To put the Nigerian society in the right perspective in respect of the qualities, attitudes and virtues which citizenship education are excepted to inculcate in the citizens: these qualities according to Asoga-Allen (2001) include honesty, tolerance, cooperation, national consciousness, patriotism, obedience to the laws (including payment of taxes in particular) consciousness and respect for fundamental human rights and freedoms: justice and fair play in inter-group and intra-group activities. Others include respect for the principles of the rule of law, free and fair elections and participation in various democratic processes and respect for informed public opinion among others. The highlighted qualities and values listed above are universally adjudged to form for harmonious co-existence and for reducing social friction to the barest minimum.

Unfortunately, however, Nigerians themselves admit that the degree of indiscipline in the society is alarming. Social vices, political and economic crimes prevail, and continue to flourish (Nwana, 1998). There is an Overgrowing frenzy by members of the public to "make it quick" and by all means. The school children no longer respect their teachers or have regard for elders or even parents: the Nigerian society is till characterized by drug addition, hard drug pushing, advanced fee fraud known as 419, cultism, rioting, poor work ethics, lateness to work, non-commitment to one's job, political victimization, embezzlement of public fund, ethnic, chauvinism, parochialism, impatient, corruption in high places and low, wrong social values religious intolerance, avarice and selfishness, ritual killing and sponsored assassination which are the social vices which citizenship education is supposed to eradicate from the society (Oyeneye, 1997).

Despite the number of years of introduction of citizenship education into Nigerian schools, the impact is yet to be felt in such a way that one could rightfully say that the national objective of the course or subject has been achieved. The values expected of citizenship education to impart in the citizens are completely absent. The following problems could be advanced for the failure of the course/subject to achieve the desired objectives. These include:

(a) Economic hardship arising from the mismanagement of the nation's economy.

(b) Political instability/military intervention in politics

(c) Poor method of teaching the subject by teachers;

(d) Restriction of the subject to senior primary classes only;

(e)   Bad leadership;

(f)   Nonchalant attitude of some parents towards moral upbringing of their children

(g)   Lack of interest on the part of the pupils; and

(h)   Inadequate facilities in Nigerian public primary schools

Economic Hardship arising from the Mismanagement of the Nation's Economy

The Nigerian economy has been badly managed over the years by some selfish leaders. It is indeed very painful when it is realized that Nigeria is an oil producing country, one of the leading oil producing nations in the world. There is nothing to show in terms of economic prosperity in the nation except high magnitude of poverty and penury ravaging the nation and its people. It is a well-known fact that Nigerian was indebted to some foreign nations to the extent that billions of dollars were being spent annually to service the debt. The level of poverty in the nation has bred a lot of social vices which are being perpetrated to the nakedness of the pupil's eyes. There is mass struggle for survival; most of them who are well to do in the country are people who have participated in impoverishing the nation. Most people struggle for what they can benefit from the nation rather than what they can contribute to the nation. There is gap between the ideals of citizenship education and the social and political realities of every day practices within the society. For example, a teacher who is tribalistic or nepotic, according to Nwayanwu (1997), cannot influence the pupils to internalize national attitudes.

Political Instability/Military Intervention in Politics

Nigeria obtained her political independence on 1st of October 1960 that is, about 55 years ago. Between 1960 till date, the military ruled for many years even though the military has no business with governance. No sooner an established civil rule was put in place than the military took over. Any time the military come to power they make proclamation that the constitutions are suspended and they start to rule by decree. This becomes inevitable because the constitution is a legal document and it would be impossible to use a legal document to perpetrate illegality.

In essence, military government is an illegal government and therefore cannot rule with the constitution. It must be stressed that one of the ideals of citizenship education is the fundamental human rights e.g. freedom from inhuman torture, freedom of speech, freedom from illegal detention, freedom to express one's opinion about the government, but during military rule, people were detained for years without being charged to court for any offence, mere expression of your opinion about the government may make one lose his life. A lot of lives were and are being terminated recklessly in the sight of the pupils. The pupils are bound to emulate what they see the society practicing that is the situation we have found ourselves today in Nigeria. Most of the social vices common to the pupils today, are borrowed from the elderly ones especially those in government.

Poor Method of Teaching Citizenship Education by Teachers

This is another major problem militating against

citizenship education from achieving the desired objectives. The way some teachers handle the subject in our primary/secondary schools, cannot help the internalization of the values of the subjects.

Nwanyawu (1997) Identified instructional strategies as the problem facing the teaching of the subject. According to him, the teachers only make use of expository, class discussion and sometimes, role playing only. Over reliance on this three methods alone without occasional taking the children out to see things themselves cannot help the achievement of the desired values, orientation and attitude formation which are pre-requisite to appropriate behaviour or are supposed to elicit appropriate behaviour response from the pupils. This problem is associated with primary and secondary school, at the tertiary level, lecture method is used. The class is usually large, because every student must pass through the course and at the end of the semester; the students are assessed in objective terms using paper and pencil. In primary school, citizenship education is not being examined at the final examination. It is only being examined at the promotional level from one class to another. According to Nwanyanwu (1997), paper and pencil assessment would not reveal whether the attitudinal change has really taken place. Hirji (1973) commenting on the way political education are impacted in Nigeria says that the atmosphere in which political education is imparted became an artificial one in which critical thought is ceremoniously banished. According to him, issues in citizenship education are moral and values questions which could not benefit those who commit them to memory. They require proper consideration, discussion, clarification, evaluation and judgment before children could take position that would form the basis of their future attitude and actions.

Restriction of the Subject to Senior Classes of Primary School

It is worth noting that Citizenship Education is only taught in the primary senior classes of the nation's primary schools. A visit to primary schools in Epe Local Government revealed that Citizenship. Education is not even being taught at all, in most of the schools. This shows the state of neglect the subject suffers in the nation's primary schools. Those schools visited could not even produce any scheme of work for Citizenship Education talk less of any textbook.

Failure to make the subject compulsory in Primary School

This is another prominent problem militating against Citizenship Education in Nigeria primary schools. Citizenship Education as a subject that educates the child about his rights, rights of other people and inculcate essential values that are needed by man to live a crisis free society, and produce a peace-loving citizens is not made compulsory in primary schools. Knowledge gained from Citizenship Education is useful for man throughout his life time. In fact, one only stops making use of the knowledge gained from Citizenship Education when he is dead. A subject like Citizenship Education is supposed to be made compulsory in the nation schools, but reverse is the case. It is natural to look down on anything that is not compulsory. That is exactly the situation Citizenship Education is going through in the nation's primary schools.

Bad Leadership

Since Independence, it is like Nigeria has not been fortunate to have a God fearing leader who could distinguish himself by leading by example. The evils perpetrated by some Nigerian past leaders cannot be forgotten as long as the nation exists. Experience has shown that corruption which Nigeria was initially rated first in the whole world and later second after Bangladesh by the Transparency International has its roots in the high places. Most Nigerian past leaders seem to place self-interest above national interest. They preferred to steal what belong to the whole Nigerians and keep it for themselves and their immediate families alone. A lot of Nigerians find it difficult to get two-square meal a day, while some past leaders are having billions of stolen Nigerian money in foreign banks. Asoga-Allen (2000) commenting on the level of corruption of the past and present Nigerian leaders says:

> *"I am yet to discover any American or Briton or any Whiteman who embezzled money in his own country and brought it to Nigerian bank or any African bank, but since the inception of self-government in Nigeria, rarely can we find any regime in which people did not steal the nation's money and deposit it in various banks abroad".*

Asoga-Allen stressed further that while majority of Nigerian are wallowing in poverty, the white men are loaning Nigerian money deposited in their banks to their people thereby developing their economy. If the leadership is corrupt and undisciplined, what do you expect of the followers? The era of which people values their names more than money in a traditional Nigerian society seems to have gone, it has been replaced by a new era where people are ready to commit any atrocity just to be rich overnight. All the evils the leaders perpetrated e.g. killing of political opponents by poisonous tea, by chemical by hired assassins, by letter bombs, by killer squad and all forms of corruption and immorality of some past leaders are being imitated by the children since they hear and see all that are happening in the society.

Nonchalant Attitude of Some Parents towards Moral Upbringing of Their Children

This is another chronic problem militating against citizenship education from achieving the desired objectives. Some parents are not disciplined, so they cannot discipline their children. Others that would have maintained discipline are faced with the struggle to make ends meet and thus, have no time to stay at home to inculcate the necessary discipline in their children. It is important to stress that for a child to be morally inclined and loyal to his nation, parents have a role to play. The type of parent determines the nature of children. A father who is an armed robber would certainly produce armed robber among his children; Likewise are all other vices like lying, evasion of taxes, duping of people, killing to mention a few.

Most pupils are not interested in citizenship education because they are aware that it is not a compulsory subject. Another reason is that pupils seem not to believe most of what the teacher teaches in citizenship education since the societal events tend to negate the ideals of citizenship education as observed by Cooksey (1981), when he comments that:

> *"One major problem of political socialization is of course the polity itself, political event and practices have far great cognition and values on students or (anyone else) than the exhortation of a civic primer"*

Cooksey stressed further that attempts to mould the minds of school goers or anyone else are bound to fail as long as, they are connected to real changes in policy.

The societal events especially during the military regime tend to make the teacher of citizenship education a mere preacher whose doctrines are not practicable. When you say something even at the tertiary level, students would tell you that "are not practicable in Nigeria".

Inadequate Facilities in Nigerian Public Primary Schools

It is a conspicuous fact that most public primary/secondary schools in Nigeria lack some major facilities necessary for the teaching of citizenship education. For example, it is not common to see any public primary school that owns a bus. Even common teaching aids like television and video machine are lacking in the public primary schools. Under this prevailing situation, to convey the pupils to places where they would see the real situation becomes difficult. This is more so since the parents seems unwilling to participate in financing education in Nigeria because of the economic problem. What the teacher does, is to confine the pupils into the classroom and discuss things which the pupils do not see physically, some of which the pupils would easily forget.

Recommendations towards Overcoming the Problems Facing Citizenship Education in Nigerian Primary/Secondary Schools

The following recommendations would help in alleviating the problems facing the achievement of the objectives of citizenship education in Nigerian primary schools:

(a)   As a matter of urgency, the subject should be made compulsory in the primary/secondary schools. In addition, the subject should form part of the final paper in Basic School Certificate/Senior Secondary Certificate Examinations.

(b)   Government should provide adequate facilities to the nation's schools to enable the teachers of citizenship education teach the subject in such a way that pupils would internalize the values.

(c)   The nation's leaders should lead by example, and shun all of form of corruption and placement of self-interest above the national interest.

(d)   Pen robber should face equal punishment commensurable to that of armed robbers, this is because robbery is robbery, whether it Is committed by armed or by pen, as both can ultimately lead to death of the person or persons robbed. In fact, the economic hardship facing most Nigerians today was caused by people who used pen to rob the nation of billions of dollars. And those people walk freely in our midst displaying their ill-gotten wealth.

(e)   Parents should be made to face some kind of humiliation and disgrace when their children are caught in a serious crime like murder, robbery, advanced fee fraud (419) etc. This step would reawaken the parents to handle the issue of moral upbringing of their children very serious (Asoga-Allen, 1998).

(f)   Parent should be morally disciplined so as to produce children who would imbibe the principle of morality. This is so, because a child would certainly imitate the parents in whatever they do, whether good or bad.

(g)   Primary school teachers as well as teachers at all levels of the nation's education should be well paid and their conditions of service should be attractive to encourage them to do their work properly. This is so because the roles of teachers in inculcating the societal values in the young ones are indispensable, and also for any educational policy to be successful, teachers must be committed and be carried along.

(h)   The nation's economy should be properly managed to eradicate poverty from the society, this is because a hungry man is an angry man. Poverty can lead someone to commit crime as it is the case now in Nigeria. Higher institution students/graduates are now being caught in armed robbery when they cannot secure a job after graduation.

In conclusion, something must be done urgently to arrest the ugly situation of the nation in which the level of insecurity is so alarming and the magnitude at which people commit crimes is so high. Citizenship Education is the appropriate subject that can be used to build a peaceful society devoid of criminality and criminally-minded people, but to achieve this, a lot need to be done by adults in the society by making themselves an epitome of morality and a model for the young ones to imitate.

Also, the leaders must turn over a new leaf and live a transparent life by making accountability and probity their guiding principles.

10.8 Citizenship Education Methodology in Primary/Secondary Schools

Introduction

Teaching is only worthwhile when it brings about desirable learning. For teaching to bring about learning with easy on the part of the learner, the teacher has to display his skilfulness by making use of the appropriate method. Practical knowledge of the subject matter is one of the ingredients of successful teaching, not the total requirement for teaching. In essence, a result-oriented teaching owes much to usage of appropriate method. Application of ideal methodology in teaching is the professional aspect of teaching that differentiates teaching from an act that is based on trial and error.

Teaching is an avenue for teacher to test his professional ability and capability. It goes beyond coming into the class to display one's grammatical prowess as thought by untrained teachers. A good teaching brings good results.

A teaching is said to be good and result-oriented when it takes into cognizance all the necessary ingredients needed for Successful teaching. These ingredients include sound knowledge of the subject matter, using of appropriate instructional materials, understanding or ability to study the students psychologically during teaching so as to know when a student is active participant in the lesson or inactive participant, adoption of appropriate teaching methodology, and ability to make the lesson achieve the pre-stated objectives.

Something is bound to happen at the end of a lesson, it is either the lesson is successful or failed. A lesson is successful when the learner is able to carry out pre-stated actions which were already stated in form of instructional objectives or behavioural objectives. The lesson is said to be a failure when the learners are unable to do what the teacher says they will be able to do at the end of the lesson.

When a lesson ends up in failure most teachers blame the learners, whereas, the fault may be from the teacher. Blaming students for inability to achieve teaching objectives is common with the untrained teachers. Sometimes, they would carry cane and start to beat the students. That is not to say that the fault cannot come from the students sometimes, but in most cases, the teacher may be the cause.

The teaching done by untrained teacher is based on "trial and error" and more often than none may fail. As observed by 'Asoga-Allen (1988)' an untrained teacher would find it difficult to control the controllable variables in the classroom because he lacks the knowledge of psychology of education, sociology of education and other foundational courses that enhance successful teaching.

Method of teaching is likened to technology in science. That is, method of doing something. When this is followed, you produce the accurate product, but when you lack the technology, you may be unable to produce the exact product.

This paper therefore, focuses on the concept of teaching concept of Citizenship Education, national objective of citizenship education, appropriate methods for teaching Citizenship Education as well as the rationale for teaching Citizenship Education.

What is teaching?

Dalen and Brittel (1999) defined teaching as the guidance of pupils through planned activities so that they may acquire the richest learning possible from their experience. They also add that learning is the result of experiences and requires the active participation of the child. In order words, the pupils do not learn merely because they have been exposed to a teacher's knowledge, to the content of textbooks, to visual aids or to laboratory equipment. Rather, learning is an active process which goes on within the pupils by guiding his leaning experiences through planned activities.

Clark and Star (1967) defined teaching as an attempt to help someone acquire or change some skills, attitudes, knowledge, ideas or appreciation. Success in teaching according to Okorie (1979), is measured by the degree to which the teacher is able to achieve the desired learning in his pupils. Okorie's opinion is shared by Asoga Allen (2000) when he comments that:

> *"In any educational system, there are two indispensable factors that need be handled with adequate care. These are the teacher and the learner, for the learning to be thorough and achieve the desirable objectives, the teacher must be ready to teach and the learners must be ready to learn. The magnitude of learning depends on the ability of the teacher to effectively, efficiently and professionally pass his message across to arouse the interest of the learners."*

In order to achieve the objectives of teaching, the teacher must know the type of learning needed by his pupils and how to bring about such learning. Teaching according to Olaitan and Agusiobo (1981) is never an easy endeavour as many teachers have taught. It involves teacher's competence in:

1. Understating children's development and learning problem;

2. Classroom management;

3. Adequate knowledge of subject matter and aims of the curriculum;

4. Use of instructional materials and techniques;

5. Improvement of instructional strategies to meet the changing demands of students for occupational knowledge and efficiency, and preparation for citizenship.

The main objective of teaching is to achieve learning. Any teaching that is devoid of learning is a wasteful exercise. It takes telling, listening, watching and active participation of the students for learning to take place. The belief is that if the teacher shows the learner how to do something or tells him how to do something that teaching has been done, does not hold water tight.

Teaching is an act, but at the same time, it does demand skills and understanding from many fields which tends to make it scientific in nature. Some of these fields are psychology, sociology, history, to mention a few. Skills and understanding from other fields is what makes teaching both an art and science.

The National Objectives of Citizenship Education

According to Asoga-Allen (2001), no nation would want its citizens to be hooligans, armed robbers, murderers, law breakers, Fraudsters, religious fanatics, terrorist, indolent, ineffective and unreliable. Thus, the national objectives of citizenship education include:

1. To create awareness of the Nigerian constitution and the need for democracy in Nigeria.

2. To introduce Nigerians to the functions and obligations of the government.

3. To create adequate and functional political literacy among the people.

4. To make Nigerians fully aware of their rights

and duties and to respect the rights of others.

5. To assist in the production of responsible, well informed and self-reliant Nigerian citizens.

6. To inculcate the right values e.g. honesty, integrity, hardworking faithfulness, fairness, and justice, to foster attitude of togetherness, comradeship and cooperation and norms for the development of individual and Nigerian society.

7. To inculcate the concept of authority, leadership and fellowship into the citizens.

8. To participate meaningfully in discussion on the Nigerian system of government and electoral process, arms of government, Code of conduct for public officers and the roles of mass media national development.

9. To articulate our history, national symbols, people and cultures of Nigeria; and

10. To discuss the characteristic features of the Nigerian environment as well as the roles of national and international Conservation

agencies.

The Rationale for Teaching Citizenship Education in Nigerian Primary School

Asoga-Allen (2003), observes that if the children are well informed about what the society cherishes and detests, and the consequences of doing them they would not like to break the laws. For example, a child needs to be told that killing is a capital offence and whoever kills another person would be killed. Not only this, other offences like stealing, fighting, lying, cheating, thuggery, disregarding traffic rules, failure to pay tax, falsification of document or information, to mention a few, could land one in jail.

Many Nigerians are in prison today for an offence they did not commit deliberately but due to ignorance of the law. It is a basic fact that ignorance is not excuse in the law court. At the same time, an accused is presumed innocent until his case has been proved beyond reasonable doubt. The judge cannot set anybody free because he is an ignorant of the law for which he was charged to court.

Ignorance is very expensive, in fact, more expensive

than education. That is why it becomes imperative for every nation to ensure that her citizens are well informed and freed from the bondage of ignorance, diseases and dogmatism. To do this, citizenship education remains an indispensable instrument.

The earlier the better, pupils of primary school would exhibit the culture of obedience to the laws rules and regulations of the society if citizenship education is properly taught. It is true that religion his a role to play in instilling morality in the citizens, but some people refrain from committing crimes not because they fear God, but because of fear of punishment. The Holy Bible supports it that one should teach his child the way he should go and when he has grown up, he would not depart from it.

In conclusion, citizenship education would undoubtedly restore sanity in Nigerian society and produce a generation of enlightened citizens who know their rights from their lefts, and who are conscious of their rights and the rights of others, and who are above board in terms of obedience to the societal rules and regulations, if properly taught in primary school.

Methods of Teaching Citizenship education in Primary School

By methods of teaching, we mean the various ways by which teachers can impart knowledge of citizenship education to the pupils. The main business of teachers in the process of teaching any subject in the curriculum is to bring about desirable learning in the pupils. The only way to quantify whether or not one's teaching has been successful is to determine whether learners have actually learned what one intended them to learn or produce a result of a clear-cut set of objectives (Asoga-Allen, 2002).

Teaching methods as earlier mentioned are the means or strategy employed by teacher in an attempt to impart knowledge to the learners.

As a matter of fact, the method employed in the classroom by teachers should depend on the situation of the class, that is, the size of the class, the ages of the pupils, maturity, and so on and so forth. However, the following methods would be of innumerable value to teachers in using them to teach citizenship education in primary/secondary schools. These include:

(a)   Discussion method

(b)   The expository method

(c)   Inquiry method

(d)   Resource person

(e)   Excursion or educational visit

(f)   Audio-visual method

(g)   Role playing

Discussion Method

This is a method in which the teacher is expected to assume or play the roles of a moderator, leader and participant. In this situation, some pupils have been selected and briefed on the topic to discus. The main task of the pupils selected into discussion group is to communicate with others and the method provides the learner with opportunity to assimilate information through the use of listening and observational process. Apart from providing opportunity for pupils to be exposed to other ideas, discussion provides opportunity for pupils to shape their own. This method would develop in pupils good social attitude such as cooperation, tolerance, self-directions, leadership, self-reliance, courtesy, taking of turns and respect for others, ideas. For an effective class discussion, the pupils must have been informed about the topic and adequate preparation must have been made by them. The teacher should round up the discussion in form of summarizing what the discussants have said, and find out from the audience whether they have question concerning the topic discussed. After this, teacher proceeds to evaluation that is, assessing the pupils based on the objectives of the lesson.

The Expository Method

This is a method characterized by the teacher teaching and explaining what has been prepared for the class. The pupils listen and put down some points they feel are necessary. Questions are generally entertained during the course of the teaching. This method allows teacher to explain and re-explain the essential points. Though expository method is prone to criticism because of its teacher- centeredness, nevertheless, it is the only practicable procedure that can be followed in large classes, To make this method achieve the instructional objectives, and to minimize the problem of teacher-centeredness, teacher should carry the pupils along by occasional questioning. If this is being done, pupils would reason, along with the teacher and also the mental alertness of the pupils would increase. This would facilitate learning.

Inquiry Method

In this method, teacher engages the pupils in judicious questioning to elicit rational responses. In teaching a topic like Government, teacher may ask pupils questions such as, who is government? Why do we need government in human society? What are likely to happen if there is no government in Nigeria? Etc. This approach would develop in the pupils the spirit of facts findings, reasoning and intellectualism. Teacher's role in this approach is that of questioning and correcting the mistakes of the pupils, by polishing the ideas expressed by the pupils and makes them cogent and acceptable.

Resource Person

This has to do with bringing an expert in a relevant area to teach the pupils. For example a lawyer may be invited to teach a topic like Fundamental Human Rights in Citizenship Education. This would enable the pupils to hear from the horse's mouth, since the lawyer is an expert in the field of legal education. The advantages of this according to Asoga-Allen (2000) are numerous, they include:

i.   It provides vivid and special information

ii.   It encourages a more relaxed and informal atmosphere.

iii.   It provides opportunity for team spirit.

iv.   It motivates learning and brings the school close to the community.

v.   It helps pupils to develop positive attitudes and values

vi.   It trains the pupils in the art of gathering information and widens their horizon.

In bringing a resource person to teach the pupils in citizenship education the teacher must be sure of the ability of the resource person to operate at the level of the pupils, because any attempt to operate above the level of the pupils would make the whole exercise a fiasco, as pupils would learn little or nothing. Also the teacher must be sure that the resource person would honour the invitation and at the appropriate or scheduled time.

Excursion or Educational Visit
This is another suitable and result-oriented method for teaching citizenship education. Excursion or educational visit method enables the pupils to visit places and see things themselves. When a topic like

the arms of government is being taught, pupils may be taken to the law court to witness court proceeding or the House of Assembly to see the law makers in action. The knowledge gained from such visit is more permanent in the pupil's memory rather than confining them to the classroom at all time. In fact, such visit would help in inculcating the values of the subject in the pupils than ordinary teaching in the classroom. Excursion or educational visit serves as a source of practical experience for the pupils. Teacher needs to do some preliminary work before making use of this method. In the first instance, he needs to apply to the place to be visited and receive approval from them, before visiting the place. Also, parents of the pupils need be informed in writing before taking the pupils on such an excursion. This is to enable the teacher know if there is any objection to the excursion by any parent. On the day of the excursion, the teacher must be extra-vigilant and extra-careful to ensure the safety of the pupils, under the "tort liability of teachers, the teacher would be held responsible for any negligence on his part which might result to injury or loss of life on the part of any pupil. Most public primary school teachers have not been able to use this method because of financial constraint, since most public primary schools in Nigeria lack the needed facilities to give pupils an all-round intellectual development.

Audio-Visual Method

Audio-visual instruction is a teaching technique in which the teacher employs audio-visual materials to an instruction. Included in the list of such materials are record players, cassettes, radios, slide and film strip, projectors, overhead projectors and television sets. Some important events documented in video film in the past, could be brought to the classroom with television and show to the pupils. Events like tying of a condemned armed robber to a tree or drum before execution, if shown to the pupils; many of them would hate robbery from their youthful age and vow not to commit such. The rationale for this method is the fact that effective learning begins with first-hand or concrete experience and proceeds towards more abstract experiences. It is factual that a pupil who has the advantage of reaching to well selected and wisely used media and materials can learn more effectively than one who is provided with largely verbal information. Asoga-Allen (2002) recommends certain steps for teachers making use or wish to make use of this method to teach any subject. These steps include:

a. Identify the state of the objectives to be achieved in teaching a specific topic;

b. break the topic down to sub-units;

c. select appropriate teaching materials for each sub-units, to play a variety of instructional roles to make optimum contributions to the fulfilment of the objectives formulated;

d. pre-view films and listen to recordings selected for use and take notes. Decide on how to organize the class to suit the nature of the presentation;

e. give a brief background of what the pupils expected to see or hear;

f. provide pupils with questions or guide on what to look for when each materials is in use;

g. do the presentation and follow up with class discussions; and

h. summarize the lesson.

This has to do with dramatization of a situation to show emotional reactions and marginal behaviour. Pupils are assigned roles to play and they act and imitate certain characters. This method can be used to inculcate important values in the pupils. It is used to develop insight into some problems of human relations that are difficult to obtain in any other way or to develop insight into the consequences of breaking the law. It helps to change the bad behaviours of the pupils and make them patriotic and loyal to their nation. The role of the teacher in this method is to select the problem to be solved and make the students aware of the problem to be acted out; give them time for preparation and instruct the rest members of the class to observe critically.

In conclusion, the importance of method of teaching cannot be over-emphasized, without the use of appropriate method, teacher, my beat about the bush for several hours, and at the end of the day fail to achieve the desired objective. Appropriate methods make learning permanent, and meaningful.

10.9 The Role of Citizenship Education in Conflict Prevention and Resolution for a Stabilized Democracy

Highly democratized nations of the world at one time or the other in their history had passed through difficult times. That is to say that perfection if possible in democracy, is not achievable in a day. Indeed, it requires a gradual process during which people have to learn through past mistakes and experiences. On the other way, conflict in democracy is not an aberration; it is a usual phenomenon especially with a young democracy. It is obligatory on any nation who is desirous of firmly rooted democracy to put in motion the appropriate machinery for conflict prevention and resolution, to guide against destabilization of their democratic experiment.

To ensure a functional society and guide against extinction, there is need to evolve an organ to resolve conflicts in a binding manner, defend the society against external attack or from being absorbed by another society. Protect lives and properties of all members of the society etc. The societal organ charged with the performance of these functions is called government (Asoga-Allen, 2001).

It is an incontestable fact that in every human society, people recognize the need for rules and regulations, orderliness, obedience to the societal laws, norms, values and cooperation. Also, there is no society all over the world that does not have societal goals or what it stands for. In order to ensure that people conform and work towards the achievement or actualization of the societal goals and shun the behaviour that are detrimental to the achievement of these goals necessary measures are put in place.

Laws are made to guide and refine human behaviours and direct It towards exercises that are meaningful productive and beneficial to the society. When laws are made, awareness must be created for the people to know that such laws are in existence or else such could be regarded as a trap. Ignorance on the other hand is not an excuse in the law court, which is the more reason why people should be informed and adequately informed when new laws are made.

Many people behave in conformity with the societal rules and regulations, that is, they do not kill, steal or lie not because they are religious as people thought but for the mere fact that there are laws that forbids such acts and whoever contravenes the law would face the wrath of the law by being punished. In essence, it is the fear of punishment that makes some people to be law abiding, refrain from acts that are capable of jeopardizing the interest of the society. It is a basic fact that every citizen in a state or society is expected to subject his personal interest to societal or national interest because; national interest is above individual interest.

The focus of this paper therefore, is on the concept of democracy, the concept of conflict, cause of conflict, concept of citizenship education and the role of Citizenship Education at protecting and resolving conflicts in a stabilized democracy.

The Concept of Democracy

Demos Kratis, or democracy as it is used today, means "the people rule". It is popularly defined as the government of the people by the people and for the people. It is a kind of government in which some people are empowered by the masses to represent their interest in the political business of administering, coordinating, directing and over-seeing human affairs. In a democratic society, everybody is part and parcel of the government not only because every human being is a political animal, but also due to the fact that no government came to be without the knowledge of the people.

In a democratic nation, government is run by the people of that country through election and representation. There is equality of every citizen in democracy and right to vote and make decisions. The origin of democracy can be traced back to about 2500 years ago, and the first countries of the world to practice democracy are Athens, Greece, Rome and later America.

There are many features of democracy. Most of these features are the same, but individual use variations of the main ideas. The main features of democracy which determines a true democracy are:

1. Competitive elections. There is usually more than one political party contesting for power

2. Certain established rules or procedures are always in place to guide and monitor the

behaviour of the major players.

3.   The press groups' e.g. labour union, students' union and other organizations are autonomous from government control, this is to enable them fight for people's right.

4.   The media e.g. radio, television, newspaper and magazines enjoy some degree of autonomy, this is to enable them be objective in their reporting.

5.   The representative assembly (the legislature) has some form of control over the executive but the judiciary is independent of both the legislative and executive. This is to enable it dispense justice without fear or favour.

6.   One-citizen one-vote principle is highly adhered to.

Concept of Conflict

Conflict can be conceptualized as a state of disagreement between people, groups, countries etc. It may also mean fighting or a war.

Whenever two or more individual or groups come into contact with each other, they choose to make their relationship primarily conflictual or primarily integrative (i.e. cooperative, supportive, agreed upon). If the initial relationship is primarily conflicted there will nevertheless emerged at least a few minimal strands of misunderstanding and reprocity rules of combat, or perhaps only an agreement to disagree. if on the other hand, the initial relationship is primarily integrative, it is certain that Conflict will develop — if for no other reason than through the demands of the association itself as they compete with the preferences of individuals and components groups.

According to Bernard (1957), there are some degrees of community organization or integration in the concept of conflict. If the parties in question were not in the same place at the same time, or performing two incompatible functions at the same time or cooperating to inflict reciprocal injury, there would be no conflict. Conflict may result in disruption or destruction of all or certain of the bonds of unity that may previously have existed between the disputants.

Conflicts take place between individuals, between individuals and organizations or groups, between an organization and one or more of its components part of a single organization or a group. A conflict emerges whenever two or more persons (or groups) seek to possess the same object, occupying the same space or the same exclusive position, play incompatible roles, maintain incompatible goals or undertake mutually incompatible means for achieving their purposes.

Causes of Conflict in Democracy

Basically, the following would bring about crises situation in a democratic society

a. Unequal opportunity: This is a situation whereby some citizens are ranked above the other in terms of opportunities in the society, perhaps due to their socio economic status or wealth or the political party they belong to or the tribe they come from. It is certain that any society where there is unequal opportunity, crises or conflict is bound to occur.

b. Rigging of election: In democracy, those to represent the people are picked through election. Ideally, an election of such nature needs to be free and fair. That is, represents the will of the people; where this is rigged in favour of a political party of individual, conflict would occur.

c. Bad leadership is another major cause of conflict in democracy. Where a leader, rather than rule by example exhibits selfishness or self centeredness, corruption, favouritism, tribalism or ethnicity etc, conflict would occur.

d. Poverty is another major cause of conflict. It is a condition of not being able to make ends meet. The basic necessities of life include food, clothing and shelter. Where a man is not able to meet these basic needs, his emotion and feelings about issues would be affected. Such a person or group of persons are prone to conflict. A minor issue that could be handled amicably can lead to conflict.

e. Another cause of conflict is unpopular government policy. Any government policy that affects the lives of the masses negatively or too harshly for the people to bear may result to conflict. Government owns it a duty to consider the interest of the people when taking any policy, failure to do this sometimes may be disastrous.

f. Political immaturity is another cause of conflict. If politics is not practiced with maturity, conflict may occur. Politics should not be a do or die affair. When two people run a race, one must certainly win and the other loses. The ideal thing is to accept the defeat in good faith. But some immature politicians and their followers would refuse to accept defeat. Thus, conflict would occur.

g. Religious intolerance is another likely cause of conflict. Religion is the belief in Supreme Being. It is something that is supposed to be between man and his God. The proper way to know a religious man is supposed to be through his behaviour not by the robe he puts on or the way he left his hair or bear uncut. Where there are multi-religions and the adherent of each claims that his religion is superior to the other or other religious set should not exist, conflict would occur.

h. Monopoly of power can also cause conflict. In a country where there are multi-ethnic groups and an ethnic group is laying hold to power at the expense of the others, conflict are likely to occur.

i. Inter ethnic struggle is another cause of conflict. In an environment where one ethnic group claims to be superior to the others or deprive the others of importance, recognition power, influence, etc conflict would occur.

j. Unemployment is another cause of conflict. Unemployment is a serious social evil in every human society. A jobless man is a deprived man; he is with less recognition and importance in the society. It is a deprivation that is capable of causing the deprived to show his potential negatively as a result of frustration that likely accompanies it. People like that easily join bad gangs or ethnic militia who are ready to commit illegality in the name of defending their people. One basic fact is that where majority are jobless or the number of the jobless is greater than the number of those who are working, conflict would always occur.

k. Corruption is another dangerous cause of conflict. Any country where corruption is a way of life, there would rarely be equitable distribution of resources. Rather, everybody would be talking of self and be self-centred. In such a situation, the few opportune ones use to take more than their own portion of the national cake thereby putting the majority in abject poverty and penury. A situation where people always steal from an economy to bank it in another country as it is the case with Nigeria, the economy would be getting poorer while the economy of the country where people bank their loot would be improving (Asoga-Allen, 2003).

In the light of the above, people suffering in the bondage of poverty would always conflict with each other for trivial issues. Causes of conflict in Nigeria today are more of poverty, unemployment, ethnic superiority struggle and religious fanaticism than any other factor or reason.

The Concept of Citizenship Education

Osakwe and Itejere (1993) defines Citizenship Education as the systematic process through which young people acquire or internalize the values, sentiments and norms of the society in which they live and actively get involved to ensure that the common good of the citizens of the society is catered for including resisting anti-social unguided "youthful exuberance." He explained that citizenship education involves critical thinking, political activism or inquiry plus the goals and values of a good citizen.

Ezegbe (1988) in an attempt to conceptualize citizenship education sees it as the education through which pupils in the school system will be taught about their rights, privileges, duties and responsibilities as good citizens and through which they will be encouraged to seek such rights and privileges, perform their duties and play a positive and active role in the society.

Coleman (1965) in his effort to define citizenship education sees the subject as political socialization. According to him, it is a process by which individual acquire attitudes and feelings towards the political system and towards their roles in it. He outlines what the process involved as:

*   Learning how the political system works
*   The growth of feelings (positive and negative about the system)
*   Development or non-development of a sense of competence to participate actively in politics

Asoga-Allen (2001) defines citizenship education as that education given by a state to its citizens to enable them to be conscious of their rights, duties, responsibilities and obligations in the society vis-à-vis the expected roles of the government to the people.

Looking through the above definitions, one major thing that is common to all is the issue of rights. The citizens are taught or educated to know their rights, duties and responsibilities in the state. Similar to this is the obligation of the citizens to the government. For a balanced society, rights and obligations must go pari-passu (Asoga-Allen, 2001).

Asoga-Allen stressed further that, certain qualities are expected from someone who has passed through citizenship education as a course, these include:

a.   Being conscious of his rights and the rights of others;

b.   being able to function effectively and efficiently in any private or governmental institution;

c.   possession and demonstration of political knowledge;

d.   being loyal and patriotic;

e.   putting national interest above self interest;

f.   being highly disciplined;

g.   interacting freely with the various ethnic group in the country;

h.   respecting the Constitution of the Federal Republic of Nigeria;

i.   being nationalistic in approach rather than tribalistic; and

j.   making accountability and probity his watchword in both private and public life.

If all these mentioned qualities are present in the citizens of a nation, that nation no doubt, would be a place to live in.

How to Prevent Conflicts through Citizenship Education

Conflicts prevention is desirable than conflict resolution. Conflict would be prevented if people are properly taught Citizenship Education, in that everybody would know his rights, the rights of his neighbours as well as his obligations to the government. Ignorance is a disease and that is why it is not accepted as an excuse in the law court. A lot of people are ignorant of what the law says concerning most of their actions, they do not know when they are right or wrong. A man that knows that if he kills he too would be killed would think twice before killing another person.

Citizenship Education would enable a man who is into politics to know that politics is not a do or die affair. That one wins to lose and loses to win. Also, knowledge of citizenship education is needed by government officials. It would enable them to make accountability and probity a principle. It would kill the spirit of self that is so common today in Africans. All the social evils characterizing the nation today would be wiped out if everyone is properly trained in citizenship education

There would be good government, corruption would be wiped out and there would be equal opportunity as contained in our national goals for every citizen. Unemployment and poverty would become a thing of the past. The society would be orderly. No ethnic group would now feel that another ethnic group is inferior to him or that power belongs to them alone. Market women would sell accordingly, not with the aim of cheating others.

How to Resolve Conflicts through Citizenship Education

Though there is bound to be conflicts between individuals, groups governments etc, such conflicts would not be violent and bloody if everyone has the knowledge of citizenship education. Resolution of such conflicts would be easy because the disputants would know their limit. People would not result to jungle justice when there is conflict rather, they would prefer to seek redress in the court of law. In short, with citizenship education there would be less conflict to resolve and the society would be peaceful.

In conclusion, if the high rate of conflicts in the countries today must be reduced, prevented and resolved, citizenship education must be given a pride of place in African nations, citizens must be properly taught not only to know their rights but to claim their rights and perform their obligation to the government and on the part of the government, there should be good governance, equitable distribution of resources, fairness and equity in handling the affairs of the people, openness, accountability and probity should be made a guiding principle.

10.10 Towards Making Citizenship Education to Achieve the National Objectives

It is indisputable fact that no nation could attain greatness if the level of ignorance among its citizens assumes a major proportion. Citizenship education is not only an instrument for keeping the citizens informed about the government activities but also a means of Liberating the citizens from the bondage of parochialism, self-centeredness, ethnicity, hooliganism, thuggery, favouritism, tribalism, bribery and corruption, putting one's interest above the nation's interest, injustice, cruelty oppression etc, by equipping them with the pre-requisite knowledge that would enable them to play their roles effectively and efficiently in their efforts to contribute their quotas to the national growth and upliftment. No amount of money could be too much for a nation to educate her citizens. More so, when it is realized that ignorance is more expensive more than education. It is pertinent to say that every citizen of a nation must pass through Citizenship Education and at the same time Citizenship

Education must pass through them so as to be able to practicalize the knowledge acquired from the subject in both individual's private and public life. This paper examines the concepts of discipline and Citizenship Education, the national objective of Citizenship Education; an update of indisciplinary acts in Nigerian society and problem hampering Citizenship Education from achieving the national objective. Recommendations towards making Citizenship Education from achieving the national objectives were made.

What is Discipline?

A discipline man is one who is capable of controlling himself and who has cultivated the habit of obedience to the rules and regulations guiding the society. Indiscipline is the mother of social vices which are negative and detrimental to the attainment of socio-economic, political, scientific goals of a given society. A disciplined society is one which the citizens conform to the rules and regulations of that society. The product of a disciplined society is peaceful atmosphere which is a pre-requisite to social, economic and political stability and prosperity, while the products of indiscipline society are Lawlessness, unguided statements, chaos, anarchy confusion etc, which are capable of running a nation.

The magnitude of indiscipline in Nigerian society has reached an alarming rate. Oyeneye (1997) observed that:

> *"Event with over 150 years of formal education and with almost 35 years of political independence, the country is infested with a high level of indiscipline especially among the so called educated elite"*

One of the causes of indiscipline among the youths in Nigeria is traceable to the fact that most elders are not disciplined. If a couple is not disciplined, one cannot expect their children to be disciplined. In essence, the children of a treasury looter would grow up to become a potential looter. Psychologically, children emulate their elders. Whatever, they found the elders doing, one day, they would do it. That is the more reason leadership must be by example and whoever would be appointed a leader must be a disciplined person. Anyone who has no discipline cannot lead by example. Naturally, a leader that brought a nation backward by his activities and subjected the citizens to an untold hardship as a result of his moral laxity or corrupt practices is not fit to live. His case is not different from that of armed robbers. For example, during the reign of a corrupt leader, many citizens may lose their lives because what belongs to them has been pocketed by very few people.

Robbery is robbery whether it is done by arm or biro. For indiscipline to be wiped out or reduced in Nigerian society, precedence has to be laid. That is why President Jerry Rawlings of Ghana should be commended for subjecting the past Ghanaian corrupt leaders to firing squad. As a result of Rawling's action, the issue of corruption seems to have been reduced to the barest minimum in Ghana. It is the turn of Nigeria to set precedence. This is necessary because the Nigerian society is seriously sick and the disease is corruption. Before this disease could be healed the society must undergo a surgical operation so that it could be purged, sanctified and cleansed of undesirable elements who feel that they are the pillars of the society whereas, the society see them as the enemies of progress.

Conceptualizing Citizenship Education

Osakwe and Itédjere (1993) after acknowledging the difficulty in giving a precise definition of Citizenship Education, defined Citizenship Education "as the systematic process through which young people acquire or internalize the values, sentiments and norms of the society in which they live and actively get involved to ensure that the common good of the citizens of the society is catered for, including resisting anti-social and unguided youthful exuberance". They explained that Citizenship Education "involves critical thinking, political activism or inquiry plus the goals and values of a good citizen".

Ezegbe (1988) defines citizenship education as "that education through which pupils in the school system will be taught about their rights, privileges, duties and responsibilities as good citizens and through which they will be encouraged to seek such right and privileges, perform their duties, and play a positive and active role in the society".

Coleman (1965) refers to Citizenship Education as political socialization. According to him, it is a process by which individuals acquire attitudes and feelings towards the political system and towards their roles in it. He outlines what the process involves as:

- Learning how the political system works:
- The growth of feelings (positive and negative) about the and
- Development or non development of a sense of competence to participate actively in politics.

Citizenship education is an education given to the citizens of a nation to make them conscious of their rights, duties responsibilities and obligations in the society as well as the expected roles of the government to the people. Citizenship Education aims at producing citizens who understand political and legal implication of whatever action taken by them or the government, respect the constitution, and the constituted authority, play effective roles in the political affairs of the nation, free from the bondage of ignorance and dogmatism by being able to think critically and rationally, and citizens who would not tarnish the image of the country at home and abroad.

Going through all the above definitions, one thing that is obvious and generally acceptable to all, is the fact that Citizenship Education is defined as training to become a good and enlightened citizen who according to the world book Encyclopaedia (1972), has been taught his civic rights and duties which include loyalty to the country, obedience to the law of the state, payment of national and local taxes and duties, and has learnt how to live and work together with other members of the Society in a friendly and cooperative manner".

As Niemeyer (1957) rightly pointed out, Citizenship Education is to help children to be socially intelligent members of the community. Citizenship Education finds its best application in the social context and so involves acquisition of knowledge, attitudes and skills which the student will utilize for the overall benefit of the society (Nwanyanwu, 1977).

The following are expected from citizens who have passed through Citizenship Education:

a. Conscious of his rights and the rights of others;
b. ability to function effectively and efficiently in any governmental institution;
c. possession and demonstration of political knowledge
d. loyalty and patriotism;
e. allowing the national interest to over-ride his self-interest;

f.   be highly disciplined

g.   ability to interact freely with the various ethnic groups in the country;

h.   respect the constitution of the Federal Republic of Nigeria;

i.   nationalistic in approach rather than tribalistic; and

j.   making accountability and probity their watchword in both private and public lives.

The National Objectives of Citizenship Education

Sheyin (1996) listed ten objectives of Citizenship Education they include:

i.   To create the awareness of the Nigerian constitution and the need for democracy in Nigeria.

ii.   To introduce Nigerians to the functions and obligations of the government.

iii.   To create adequate and functional political literacy among the people.

iv.   To make Nigerians fully aware of their rights and duties and to respect the rights of others.

v.   To assist in the production of responsible, well-informed and self-reliant Nigerian citizens.

vi. To inculcate the right values e.g. honesty, handwork, integrity, faithfulness, fairness and justice, to foster attitude of togetherness, comradeship and cooperation among the various people of Nigeria.

vii. To inculcate the concept of authority, leadership and followership in the citizens.

viii. To participate meaningfully in discussions on the Nigeria system of government and electoral process, arms of government, code of conduct for public officers and the roles of mass media in National development.

ix. To articulate out history, national symbols, people and cultures of Nigeria; and

x. To discuss the characteristic features of the Nigerian environment as well as the roles of national and international conservation agencies.

When the above listed objectives are achieved, the nation could boast of citizens who are highly enlightened and who are conscious of their roles whether as a group or individuals, in public or private sector and in short as Nigerians. When this happens, there would be orderliness, peace and tranquillity in the society. For example, as a citizen who is conscious of his rights and the rights of his neighbour, he would not like to infringe on his neighbour's rights so as not to lose his own rights. Because every individual is a major protector of his rights, if you do not want your rights to be disrespected, you have to respect the rights of others. The moment you abuse the rights of others or commit any crime against the state, your rights would be abused.

It could also be seen from the objectives that Citizenship Education hopes to produce citizens, who are nationalistic in actions activities rather than those who are tribalistic or ethnically minded. Also, if the objective of Citizenship Education are achieved; the society is expected to be free from corruption, religious riot, armed robbery, murder, power tussle, political immaturity, examination malpractices, thuggery, tribalism, favouritism, self-centredness, etc that have characterized the nation. Thus, it could be said that the occurrences in our society have not justified the inclusion of Citizenship Education in the nation's school curriculum. The end has not been justifying the means.

That means there are problems facing the achievement of the objectives. Worst still, is the fact that some of those in position of authority (leaders) who are supposed to exhibit and demonstrate high exemplary character both in their public and private lives are the major culprits of indiscipline in the society. Imagine the law makers being furious to the extent of throwing chairs on each other or exchanging physical combat over minor disagreement, or law makers making statements that are capable of bringing the nation's progress back to square one in public! All these and others are evidence of indiscipline and non-conformity with the ethnics of Citizenship Education.

An Update of Indisciplinary Acts in Nigeria Society

Despite the inclusion of Citizenship Education in the curriculum of the nation's primary, secondary and the tertiary institutions, it is important to note that the level of ignorance among Nigerians is still very high. Many of Nigerian politicians are politically immature. This is evident in the actions of those elected to local, state and federal legislature. Instead of cooperating with the executive by initiating and implementing policies that would alleviate the suffering of the masses and heal the wounds which the people have sustained from many years of corrupt and purposeless rules of some military leaders, they concentrate their energies on usurping the executive functions for personal gains. It is obvious from the way some of them talk and behave that they do not understand the constitution as regards the functions expected of them to performs vis-à-vis that of the executive.

It is highly ridiculous to hear a legislative member calling for military intervention or threatening to impeach the executive president for false allegations which cannot be substantiated. The legislature rather than cooperating and concentrating on their legitimate functions engaged the executive in power tussle. Any proposal by the executive that does not take the interest of the legislature into consideration, that is, their immediate benefits would rarely receive the attention of the legislature. An example is year 2000 budget presented to the legislature by President Olusegun Obasanjo since September 1999. The budget was not passed until late April, 2000.

The legislature did not only inflated the budget by including their own benefits and interest but started to trade with the budget by collecting money from some ministers with the promise of jerking up their allocations (Sunday Tribune, 16th April, 2000). Some legislators engaged themselves in actions which could be regarded as "advanced fee fraud" known as (419) by collecting N5.5 million from a minister under the pretext that his allocation would be jerked up, but the minister could not find the affected legislature when he was to defend the budget among the committee members on appropriation. And this made the minister to find it tough to defend his budget (Sunday Tribune, 16th April, 2000).

The common language which most of the legislative members seem to understand is impeachment. Both at the local, state and federal level of governments, the legislature threatened to impeach the executive over actions which seem to contradict their personal selfish ambition. An example at the federal level was the move by Arthur Nzeribe to impeach President Olusegun Obasanjo which created serious hullabaloo in the House of Senate (the Guardian, 18th April, 2000). And this move attracted condemnation from almost all Nigerians.

Coming to the level of the masses, it was problem here and there. Every ethnic group expressed frustration in one way or the other against the government or against another. An Ogoni faction group engaged another in a dwell leading to the death of about seven persons (The Guardian, Wednesday, April 12, 2000). The Ijaw youth engaged Urhobo people in a dwell in which lives were lost; Ife/Modakeke was not left out. Thousands of innocent lives and properties were wasted. Those entrusted with the security maintenance of the nation were not left out. A police inspector attached to the Federal Investigation and Intelligence Bureau (F1IB) Alagbon was arrested because the armed robbers mentioned his name as their god-father supplying them with weapons, also an Army Corporal attached to Yaba Cantonment was caught in an attempt to sell bullets to armed robbers (The Guardian, Wednesday, 12th April, 2000).

In Kaduna, the Muslims declared religious war against the Christians over the introduction of Sharia in Zamfara and the proposal to introduce same in Kaduna. This resulted into lost of lives and destruction of properties worth billions of naira (Tell, April 17, 2000).

Those who embezzled the nation's money during the

military regime were using this ill-gotten wealth to sponsor riot here and there with the intention of destabilizing the government. The reasons for this action were not unconnected with the masses-oriented programmes which the President, Chief Olusegun Obasanjo seems to be implementing in order to alleviate the problem of poverty facing the masses. Also, the anti-corruption crusade being championed by the President coupled with his loot-recovery drive from those who looted the nation's treasury during the military days in governance, were causing some past corrupt leaders a nightmare. Thus, they resulted to using their stolen wealth to frustrate the move (The Punch, 17 April, 2000). The Sharia issue which resulted to bloody war between Muslims and Christians in Kaduna was purely a political matter carried out in the name of religion. During this war thousands of innocent lives were terminated and properties worth billions of naira were destroyed (Tell, 17th April, 2000). Other tribes who were Muslims were killed.

The relationship between the legislature and the executive was nothing to write home about. From all indications, the reasons for this may be said to be connected with the failure by the executive to

Compromise with the legislature in their ambition to share what remained in the nation's treasury among themselves. This was evident in the actions of the legislature by budgeting extra 22.6billion naira to themselves in the appropriation bill without consulting the executive, also, by jerking up the allocations for some ministries after collecting money from the ministers heading such ministries (The Guardian, 17th May 2000).

Where are we heading to as nation if after 55 years of political independence, the nation is still being faced with the problem of leaders who are self-centred, corrupt and politically immature? The fact that President Olusegun Obasanjo had good intention and was determined to bring back Nigeria to her lost glory was obvious to all Nigerian, but the problem was that the president was surrounded by people whose visions and ambitions were to share the national cake among themselves and forget about the people who elected them to power and the development of Nigeria. The mentality of equating political office with amassing wealth which the people inherited from the military rule still remains with them. For instance, if President Olusegun Obasanjo had given the legislative members

5 million naira each as bribe, they would not have read through the budget before passing it, but because he did not bribe them, they decided to delay the budget for months and at the end added their own and inflated the budget.

The problem of selfishness is not limited to the federal legislature alone, at the state level; the story seems to be the same. For example, in a state, the legislature passed a bill in which they stated that 15% of the total budget for the state should be for the constituency development projects, that the money would be administered by the legislature; also the project would be supervised directly by the legislative members from each of the constituencies. This action was not only illegal and unconstitutional but tantamount to usurping the executive function for personal gain. All these excesses on the part of both federal and state legislature could be attributed to ignorance and lack of understanding of their roles vis-a-vis that of the executive.

Another serious indiscipline within Nigerian society today is the problem of policemen colleting bribe openly in public. This development is another dimension to issues of corruption in Nigeria as a nation, all pronouncements during the military regimes put an end to this misdemeanour was not followed with equal seriousness that could have made it successful. This social menace had been carried out to the civilian regime. The question is "what image are these people creating for Nigeria especially in the eyes of the foreigners?" in fact, if people do not know, it is a national disgrace.

The police represent government of Nigeria the way people see them. They are the ones entrusted with enforcing the laws of the nation. In fact, corruption is one of the criminal offences punish under the constitution of the Federal Republic of Nigeria (Nigerian Constitution, 1999). If those charged with maintenance of Law are now law breakers, where do we go to? The situation is really ridiculous looking at the ways some policemen struggle with the bus drivers/conductors in attempt to collect this N20. For example, a bus conductor was shot dead by a member of "Operation Sweep" a security outfit put up by Col. Buba Marwa, the then Military Administrator of State for failure to give N20 bribe at Isheri-Lagos (The Guardian, 29th March, 1999). There are other atrocities being perpetrated by some unscrupulous policemen e.g. armed robbery, illegal detention, supplying of arms to armed robbers to mention a few. The Army is not left out in the atrocities. However, the policemen are part and parcel of Nigerian society and what is happening in the police is a reflection of the society, but what makes the police action as regards open collection of bride more serious, is the function which they are charged to perform and the effect which open collection of bride may have on the youth.

A lot of government agencies and parastatals are more corrupt and openly displayed indiscipline than the police. Take for example, the Power Holding Company of Nigeria (PHCN). The staffs of this parastatal generate money into their individual pockets than into the government treasury. They openly collect bribe from house to house and encourage customers not to pay electricity bill by collecting bribe from them. Indeed, they become unhappy when customers settle their bills regularly. They prefer customers to owe their Corporation so that they can collect bribe from them as they like. Apart from the staff of PHCN, the management of the corporation runs the outfit to oppress Nigerians. In fact, it is difficult to believe that Nigeria is an independent nation by the way PHCN relates to their customers. When they disconnect light for months, they make customers to pay for the period they were in darkness, they bill people the way they like, and they have crazy and normal bills.

They make customer's to pay for service they did not enjoy. The worst part is that when the transformer which is their instrument of trade develops fault, the customers are made to pay for its repair. If they fail to do this, the transformers would be taken away for months and it will not be returned until the users pay something for the repair. The question is "Why should people who pay their bills be made to repair PHCN's facility?" All these account for why people see PHCN as the worst thing that has ever happened to Nigerians. The actions of the PHCN staffs make one sceptical whether actually Nigeria has obtained independence. Even during the colonial regime, people were not made to pay for what they did not buy. A lot of Nigerians would have taken the PHCN staff/management to court for one wrong doing or the other but the constitution of the country does not give room for PHCN staff/management to be sued to court, that is why they behave like tin god.

The Nigerian Custom is another government agency

where the staffs make money into their pockets. They aid and abet smugglers. Only those who fail to settle them have their goods seized. They collect bribe in thousands and millions of Naira, they ride expensive cars and build magnificent houses all about. People talk less of them because not everybody is having something to do with them, but basically, they are one of the most corrupt government agencies in Nigeria.

Another important area that must be touched when it comes to indiscipline is the rootless and lawless driving of the commercial drivers. Most of the Nigerian commercial drivers are heartless people. When you drive in most cities in Nigeria, one would hate driving because of the way Nigerian commercial drivers drive. Most accidents on Nigerian roads are caused by dangerous driving of Nigerian commercial drivers. Most Nigerian commercial drivers are so impatient, intolerant, over ambitious to make thousands of naira in a day; thus, they engage in over speeding, they drive against traffic, they stand on the road to carry passengers, they drive under the Influence of alcohol and drugs. Another set of killers in the driving sector are the trailer and tanker drivers. People see them as death because of their reckless dangerous and I don't care driving attitude.

No wonder accident is so rampant on Nigerian roads, and thousands of lives are lost to road accident annually. There were Instances where people slept on the road because of traffic jam caused by reckless and impatience of Nigerian commercial drivers. The worst is that no concerted effort on the part of the government to arrest the situation. When a driver engages in accident as a result of dangerous driving and killed all the occupants of the vehicle, and the driver survives it, he is only made to face prosecution after which he serves, i.e punishment and freed, or left out of the hook, If the driver is conscious of the fact that, he would be killed if accident occurs as a result of his carelessness, he would be careful while driving.

Another perspective to view the issue of irrational and dangerous driving of Nigerian commercial tanker drivers is to look at the personality of the drivers. Who are these drivers and what are their antecedents? In fact, most Nigerian commercial drivers are people who have been rejected by their parents due to stubbornness, unruly behaviour and disobedience. When these kinds of people are sent out by their parents, they sleep outside, under the bridge, in the market place, and later join garage workers. From this garage work, they become emergency drivers. Most of them have no home address, if they die, no one is going to find them, It is really very painful when it is realized that these are the people that engage in transport business in Nigeria. They don't mind to die. They can curse and slap somebody of their parent's age. Because of their disrespectful behaviour, some of them are cursed. They smoke Indian hemp and take alcohol before and after driving. In fact, as at today, if you are looking for touts, hooligans, thugs, disorderly people, they are found in transport sector. The politicians recruit them as thugs against their opponents during election and electioneering campaign.

Indiscipline is not limited to the areas already discussed, when you visit ministries, state or local government secretariat, and you want to see any highly placed public officer, the receptionist would expect you to bribe him before he allows you in, he would tell you his oga (boss) is busy. When you offer him something, he allows you in immediately. Most of the contracts given to the contractors in government are poorly executed perhaps because those in charge of giving out contract collect gratifications from the contractors or some percentage of the cost of the contract. In some cases, contract costs are inflated. At other times, some contracts given out and paid for, were not executed. (National Concord, 17th May, 2000). In the light of the above, it is conspicuous that Citizenship Education has not achieved much in terms of the national objectives which it has been introduced to achieve.

Problems Hampering Citizenship Education from Achieving the National Objectives

Citizenship Education is being faced with a number of problems, these include:

1. **Bad Leadership**

   Leadership is the ability to lead, when there is leadership, there must be followership. The leadership is the mirror in which members of the society see themselves, whatever habit the leaders are fond of, would definitely be emulated by the followers especially when it comes to discipline and indiscipline. Nigerian as a nation has been unfortunate when it comes to having a good leader that is filled with mission, vision and determination to serve the people rather than to promote his self-interest.

Political records have shown that the most sensitive atrocities being perpetrated in Nigerian society come from the leaders. For example, if it has been possible for some past military leaders to convert Nigeria to their private property, they would have done so. According to Sunday Tribune of 16th April, 2000. The greatest looting in the world history was carried out in Nigeria between 1988 and 1993. It is believed strongly that the leaders of the time cannot be exonerated from the six billion dollar-loot, in fact, one may rightly say that some of the leaders introduced all the atrocities booming in Nigerian society today e.g. fraud, termination of innocent lives, funding religious riot etc. Though, there is a constitution for the Federal Republic of Nigeria which stipulates the dos and don'ts but the leaders had not been following the constitution. If a leader is engaging in all sorts of criminality, what do you expect of the followers.

2. **Military Intervention in Politics**

Another problem hampering Citizenship Education from achieving the national objectives was the constant military intervention in Nigerian politics. The constitution of the Federal Republic of Nigeria does not give room for military governance. Anytime military takes over power they accuse the regime overthrown of one wrong doing or the other. They use to give the impression that they have come to put things right, but at the end they would do worse.

The first-step anytime military comes to power is to suspend the constitution and start to rule by decrees, when this happens, the society become abnormal society. In a situation like that both the government and his activities are against the ideals of Citizenship Education. For example, the fundamental human rights as entrenched in the 1989 constitution of Federal Republic of Nigeria excludes every citizens of Nigeria from illegal detention, and allows for freedom of speech for every citizen.

But during military rules, all these rights were withdrawn and people are subjected to inhuman treatment, illegal detention etc, It is worthy of note that any time there is military rule, the students would never benefit or assimilate whatever Citizenship Education teacher/Lecturer teaches because the ideals contained in Citizenship Education are contrary to the military government structure and event of the society during military rule.

3. **Crazy for Luxury**

This is another problem hampering achievement of the objectives of Citizenship Education in Nigeria. Nigerians love luxury too much and they want to make it by all means. The society worship those who have made it, gone are the days when people bother to know the source of wealth of a person before giving him respect. Nowadays, people do not bother if one is an armed robber provided he has the money, they would worship him and give him their daughter to marry.

4. **Inadequate Facilities in Schools**

This is another problem, Citizenship Education is taught in the nation's primary, secondary and the tertiary institutions and if the subject/course is to be properly taught, there is need for adequate facilities. The pupils/students needs to interact with the real situation so as to internalize the values, But in our educational institutions pupils/students are confined to the classrooms due to unavailability of school bus to convey them on excursions. According to Nwanyanwu (1977), the students are assessed with paper and pencil which would not reveal whether the attitudinal change has really taken place. As a result of inadequate facilities pupils/student, only commit what they are taught into memory just for examination purpose. And as observed by Hiriji (1973) "issues in Citizenship Education are moral and value questions which could not benefit those who commit them to memory, they require proper consideration, discussion, clarification, evaluation and judgment before students could take positions that would form the basis of their future attitude and actions.

5. **Curriculum Deficiency**

The Curriculum of Citizenship Education is not wide enough. For example, 'the constitution" as a topic under Citizenship Education does not contain the criminal offences and their penalties. Some people committed some offences not deliberately but because they were ignorant of their actions. Thus, there is need to include some illegal acts and their penalties in the curriculum. This would further enlighten the pupils/students because ignorance is not an excuse in law.

6. **Teachers Poor Condition of Service**

The condition of service of Nigeria teachers is not something to write home about. Apart from the fact that Nigerian teachers are not well paid, their salaries are not promptly paid. In some states, teachers get their pay after all their counterparts in the ministries might have been paid. The economic hardship has actually affected some teachers that they find it difficult to feed their families and pay their house rents. This situation has forced many teachers into becoming petty contractors, pool takers, etc, which seems to distract their attention from concentration on their job. Others have resulted to collecting illegal fees from pupils and engaging in all sorts of illegalities just to make the ends meet. If the teachers who are the immediate leaders to the pupils cannot show leadership by example, how would they impart necessary moral values into the pupils/students?

7.   **Neglect of Our Culture**

As a result of introduction of western education and the infiltration of foreign culture into Nigeria through uncontrolled importation of foreign films, Nigerians have given up their culture. The eyes of most Nigerians seem to have been negatively opened, thus, they seem to see their traditional culture as uncivilized like the foreign ones. Everybody wants to be like Whiteman or woman hence, the various social vices associated with the foreign culture in Nigerian society.

Recommendation toward Making Citizenship Education Achieve the National Objectives

The following recommendations would assist in

ensuring a result oriented Citizenship Education in Nigerian educational institutions and help in the achievement of the national objectives

1. The curriculum of Citizenship Education should be widened to incorporate types of offences and their penalties. This would liberate citizens from the bondage of ignorance as regards most of their actions that are against the law.

2. There should be political education for those at the legislative arm of the nation's government from time to time to acquaint them with their roles, limitations as well as the roles and prerogative of the executive.

3. Government should provide our schools with all the necessary facilities to enable teachers teach Citizenship Education properly.

4. Teachers Salary Scale (TSS) should be paid to teachers in full because of the nature of their job as nation builders. And government should do all what is possible to encourage and motivate teachers to do their job effectively and efficiency through enhanced welfare packages.

5. Nigerians generally should stand firm against military intervention in politics and should never accept military back into Nigerian politics no matter the excuses given.

6. The masses should be educated or enlightened on the need to shun money politics as this would only make the nation retrogress rather than progress.

7. Equality before the law as guaranteed by the principles of the rule of law should be enforced in Nigeria. Any corrupt leader or incredible public or private officer should be made to face the consequences of his behaviour.

8. Those past leaders who have ploughed the nation to the present economic disaster by looting the nation's treasury should be tried and the looted money recovered from them. Also they should not be recognized in the society. In this respect, the idea of giving chancellorship appointment to some ex-presidents who were major factors in the nation's economic woes is not welcomed.

9. The President should not waste time in arresting those using their ill-gotten wealth to sponsor crises throughout the nation — as delay may be dangerous.

10. The President should strive to do good work and not hesitate to expose all who are seeking his compromise to loot the nation. This is more necessary because, he is the one that God has put there as the head, he should play his role creditably so as to have his name written in gold on earth and in heaven.

11. The legislators who contested the election with the aim of impoverishing the nation for self-enrichment should be warned. They should be conscious that Nigeria of today is different from that of the past, eyes are seriously on them and Nigerians would not let them go scot free if they failed the nation.

12. Nigerians should not welcome any impeachment of the executive based on trivial or selfish reason. When there is any mistake on

the part of the executive, it should be corrected through dialogue.

13.   All Nigerians should be enlightened that no nation could attain economic, political and social height if its citizens are corrupt, self-centred and selfish. Also, there is the need to screen seriously those that would be elected as leaders to represent the people.

14.   All those ex-leaders found guilty of corruption and those who have served in their corrupt governments and still serving in the present regime should be relieved of their posts as a matter of urgency while new people should be injected to serve their people.

15.   The Nigerian police should be reformed and re-organized; all the bad eggs who refuse to change for better and are still carrying wrong mentality should be flushed out. If the Nigerian police are still collecting money openly on our highways and abusing the power given to them by the Constitution by exploiting the masses, people would make mockery of corruption

crusade of the federal government.

16. Government should take a decisive step by engaging on mass retrenchment of PHCN staff (from the top down the leader) and inject new blood (people). Even the newly recruited ones should be monitored with intelligent agents so as to fish out and arrest those of them who are corruptly infected. This becomes very important if government really want to fight corruption. The action of PHCN staff constitutes highest indiscipline and it's capable of corrupting Nigerian youths.

17. Government should stop wastages of human Jives by carrying out instant reform of the transport sector. Those to be commercial trailers/tanker drivers should possess a minimum of West African School Certificate and must collect a letter of attestation from a reputable traditional ruler in their area or their parents. And any driver who survives an accident in which people lost their lives and were caused by dangerous driving should be killed not imprisoned.

18.   On crises here and there, government should take more decisive action against any community where this happens. The State Security Service (SSS) should be encouraged to do their work more effectively so as to detect the root of the crises. If evidence of sponsoring crises is established against anybody, no matter how highly placed in the society, he should be tried for treasonable felony and the law should take its course. The situation now does not show that the SSS are performing or allowed to perform. If they are really performing, most of the crises taking lives and properties would have been detected before implementation and those responsible would have been arrested.

19.   Nigerians should cooperate and support only masses-oriented government programmes.

REFERENCES

Adebamowo, O. (1996) (Eds) Citizenship Education. Abeokuta: Gbemi Sodipo Press.

Adefolarin, A. (1981) Political Scheme and Government of West Africa. Lagos: Academic Press Ltd.

Adegoke, O. O. et al (1996) (eds) General Studies for Higher Education. Modakeke: Decency Printers and Stationery Ltd.

Agagu, A. A. (1993) Rights and Obligations of Citizens in a State. In Odusina, S. A. and Tella, P O. (eds) Citizenship Education. Abeokuta, Gbemi Sodipo Press.

Asoga-Allen, K. (1999) Private Participation in Nigeria Education System: A Means of Restoring Confidence in Nigerian Education. The Beagle, vol. 3

Asoga-Allen, K. (2000) Professionalization and improvement of Teacher's Condition of Service: A Pre-requisite for achievement of Success in UBE Programme. School of Science Publication, Adeniran, Ogunsanya College of Education, Otto Ijanikin.

Asoga-Allen, K. (2001) Nigerian Society and Citizenship Education. A Journal of institute of Education, LASU, Epe

Asoga-Allen, K. (2001) Citizenship Education for Tertiary Institutions. Ijebu-Ode: Fembol Intergra Nig. Ltd.

Asoga-Allen, K. (2003) Citizenship Education in Primary School. In Viatonu, O. and Osisami, F.R. (eds) Fundamentals of Education. Ijebu-Ode: Lucky Odoni Nig. Ent.

Asoga-Allen, K. (2003) General Studies in Education: Political Economy Science and Society. Ijebu-Ode: Lucky Odoni Nig. Ent.

Bernard, J. (1957) Parties and Issues in Conflict. Journal of Conflict Resolution. 1-11-121.

Clark, L. J. and Star, I. S. (1967) Secondary School Teaching Methods. New York: Macmillan Press.

Coleman, J. S. (1965) (ed) Education and Political Development. Princeton NIJ: Princeton University Press.

Collin, O. H. (1983) Harraps Mini Pocket English Dictionary. London: Harrap Limited.

Dalen, D. E. and Britel, R. W. (1999) Looking Ahead to Teaching. Boston: Allyn and Vaccon

Ezegbe, M. O. (1988) Foundations of Social Studies. Umuahia: Publishers.

Federal Republic of Nigeria (1960) Independence Constitution of Federal republic of Nigeria. In Odusina, S. A. and Tella, P. O. (eds) Citizenship Education. Abeokuta: Gbemi Sodipo Press

Federal Republic of Nigeria (1963) Republican Constitution of the Federation. In Odusina S. A. and Tella P. O. (eds) Citizen Education. Abeokuta: Gbemi Sodipo Press.

Federal Republic of Nigeria (1979) constitution of Federal Republic of Nigeria. Lagos: NERDC Press.

Federal Republic of Nigeria (1979) Constitution of Federal Republic of Nigeria. Lagos: NERDC Press.

Federal Republic of Nigeria (1999) Constitution of Federal Republic of Nigeria. Lagos: Federal Government Press.

Hijiri, K. F. (1973) School Education and

Underdevelopment. In "Tanzania" Maji Maji no. 12. 12— 1

Logman Dictionary of Contemporary English (1995) (Third Edition) Great Britain: Glays Ltd.

National Concord, 17th May, 2000

Niemeyer, J. H. (1957) Education for Citizenship in Henry, N. B. (ed) Social Studies in Elementary Schools: The Fifty-Sixth Year book of Education on Part II. Chicago: University of Chicago Press

Nwanyanwu, O. J. (1997) Managing Ethnic Conflict and Violence in Nigeria Through Citizenship Education. In Nwanyanwu, O. J. et al (eds) Education for Socio-Economic and Political Development in Nigeria. Abeokuta: Visual Resources.

Okorie, J. U. (1979) Fundamentals of Teaching Practice. Enugu: Fourth Dimensional Publishing Company Ltd.

Olaitan, L. and Agusiobo, C. (1981) in Asoga Allen K. (1999) improving Students' Teaching Practice Exercise in Teacher's Colleges. Academic Review. Vol. 2, No. I

Osakwe, E. O. and Itedjere, F. O. (1993) Social Studies for Tertiary Students in Nigeria. Enugu: New Age Publishers.

Oyeneye, O. Y. (1997) Education as an Instrument of Socio-Economic and Political Development. In Nwanyanwu, O. J. et al (eds) Education for Socio-Economic and Political Development In Nigeria. Abeokuta: Visual Resources.

Sheyin, A. O. (1996) "The Concept of Constitution. In Omolade Z. A. and Adebamowo, 0. (eds) Citizenship Education. Ijebu-Ode: Dapo Educational Publishers.

Sheyin, A. O. (1994) The Concept of Constitution. In Z. A. Omolade and Adebamowo, O. (eds) Citizenship Education. Abeokuate: Gbemi Sodipo Press.

Sunday Tribune, 16th April2000

Tell, 17thApril, 2000

The Guardian, 12th April2000

The Guardian, 18th April 2000

The Guardian, 17thApril 2000

The Punch, 17th May 2000

World Book of Encyclopedia (1972) Chicago. Field Enterprises Educational Corporation. Vol 4.

Index

E

F

J

K

L

M

V

www.ingramcontent.com/pod-product-compliance
Lightning Source LLC
Chambersburg PA
CBHW071336280526
45787CB00001B/116